The Theory and Interpretation of Narrative Series

A Glance beyond Doubt

Narration, Representation, Subjectivity

Shlomith Rimmon-Kenan

Ohio State University Press
Columbus

Library of Congress Cataloging-in-Publication Data

Rimmon-Kenan, Shlomith
    A glance beyond doubt : narration, representation, subjectivity /
Shlomith Rimmon-Kenan.
       p. cm. — (The theory and interpretation of narrative series)
    Includes bibliographical references and index.
    ISBN 0-8142-0706-5.
    1. Mimesis in literature. 2. Subjectivity in literature. 3. Narration
(Rhetoric) I. Title. II. Series.
PN56.M536R56 1996
801'.95—dc20   96-13704
                                                    CIP

Text design by John Delaine.
Type set in Sabon and Gill Sans.
Printed by Thomson-Shore, Dexter, MI.

9 8 7 6 5 4 3 2 1

To my children, Avi and Yael

Contents

Acknowledgments

Although chapters 2, 3, and 4 are substantially different from the articles I published on those texts, I wish to acknowledge permission to use the original material, parts of which remain unchanged. The early version of chapter 2 was published in *Degrés* 16 (1978) under the title "From Reproduction to Production: The Status of Narration in Faulkner's *Absalom, Absalom!*" Chapter 3 is based on "Problems of Voice in Vladimir Nabokov's *The Real Life of Sebastian Knight*," *Poetics and Theory of Literature* 1 (1976). Chapter 4 first appeared as "Ambiguity and Narrative Levels: Christine Brooke-Rose's *Thru*," *Poetics Today* 3 (1982).

I am deeply grateful to the then Rector, now President, of the Hebrew University, Hanoch Gutfreund, and to the former Dean of Humanities, Amnon Linder, for granting me leaves of absence at two different but equally crucial periods of the writing.

No thanks can sufficiently acknowledge my debt to Dorrit Cohn, Bill Daleski, and Michal Govrin, all of whom read the whole manuscript with a wonderful combination of friendly encouragement and honest, acute criticism. They pointed out weaknesses in the argument from different perspectives and often suggested directions for improvement. I also owe much to Ruth Ginsburg for a continuous dialogue as well as for invaluable comments on various parts of the manuscript. Susan S. Lanser made stimulating and far-reaching comments on an earlier version of the book, causing me to rethink and clarify many of my positions.

Ruth Nevo contributed an important insight for the development of my thinking, and Gershon Shaked provided illuminating analysis of a specific impasse. Menakhem Brinker and Leona Toker were very helpful about certain theoretical problems. Warm thanks are due to my students both at the Hebrew University and at Harvard University. Their unfailing interest and critical challenges in courses related to this book have forced me to modify my views and refine my readings. My highly intelligent research assistant at Harvard, Martha Nadell, was very helpful in reviewing the theoretical literature. Last but not least, I want to express my gratitude to the editors of the Theory and Interpretation of Narrative Series at Ohio State University Press, as well as to the Press's external reader, for their reports. I have profited immensely from these in reexamining some of my main contentions and making final revisions.

The chapter on *Beloved* was the germ of the whole project, and I am grateful to Ruth Nevo, who stimulated my lasting interest in Morrison's work. Bennett Simon's analysis of the connection between the murder of children and the killing of storytelling in *Tragic Drama and the Family* has greatly influenced my consideration of the opposite phenomenon. Elizabeth Freund made thought-provoking comments on the first draft, as have the many colleagues who heard it at Princeton, Berkeley, Santa Cruz, and Nice. My special thanks go to Toni Morrison herself for patiently listening to my presentation at Princeton in 1990 and engaging in an extremely illuminating dialogue, whose echoes reverberate in chapter 6.

Two periods of escape from daily pressures into paradise-like working conditions have proved particularly fruitful. I am immensely grateful to Dorrit Cohn (again) and to Lore and Wolfgang Iser for their generous hospitality.

My greatest debt of gratitude is to my husband and children, without whose love and support this book could not have been written.

A Note on Terminology

The traditional assumption that language and literature can and do mirror or reflect reality was often associated with the Aristotelian term *mimesis*. Later claims about the limitations of language and literature have, among other things, led to a substitution of *representation* for *mimesis*. Since I am fully aware of the problematic nature of language and literature, I use *representation* consistently in my discourse, but I retain *mimesis* both in quotations from others and in references that are meant to evoke the traditional belief in imitation. A similar procedure characterizes my use of *self* and *subject*. The traditional humanist conception of an autonomous, introspective self has often been contested, leading to a replacement of *self* by *subject*.[1] The view I suggest incorporates the interrogation of the traditional one, and I use *subject* rather than *self* except in quotations or when referring to the concept in its humanist acceptation. I also use *self* in the chapter on *Beloved,* because in that novel the term recurs in dramatizing the painful aspirations of subjects to become selves.

Introduction

In this book I have two main concerns. Conceptually, I attempt to reinstate representation and rehumanize subjectivity—not by returning to traditional humanist perspectives, but by integrating the contemporary destabilization of these concepts and going beyond that destabilization by viewing narration as access. Historically, I trace a parallel movement—from conflict to dismantling to a tentative rehabilitation—in the Anglo-American novel of our century. The relation I establish between the two concerns is not an application of a theoretical hypothesis to works of literature or a corroboration of the hypothesis by them, nor is it only an analogy between conceptual and novelistic grapplings with the same issues. Rather, I endeavor to theorize through literature, to use the novels as, in some sense, the source of theory. After all, "the poets were there before us," as Freud remarked. However, it goes without saying that a reading of the novels with certain emphases in mind presupposes at least an implicit conceptual framework. The circularity this creates can be seen as a fruitful dialogue or interaction between literature and theory, a beneficent spiral rather than a vicious circle.

Throughout the history of philosophy, linguistics, psychoanalysis, and literary theory, the terms *representation* and *subjectivity*

(or their earlier versions, *mimesis* and *self*)[1] have given rise to opposed views, each of which presented itself as excluding the other.
Deconstruction has tried to dismantle the principle of binary opposition, but its perception of the mutual generation of opposites
is firmly rooted in the same kind of dichotomous thinking.[2] Theories of ideology inspired by Althusser and Foucault offer a way
out of the dichotomy only at the cost of assumptions severing any
relation to reality and self and rendering meaningless the very
question of the possibility or impossibility of representation and
subjectivity. My own suggestion of a way out is an attempt to
shift the ground of the discussion, to understand the concepts
within a different analytical framework.

Most disagreements about representation and subjectivity are
based on postulating one of two relations between words and
things: reference (involving a truth-claim of sorts)[3] or specularity
(mirroring, reflection, correspondence, similarity, verisimilitude).
According to one polar view, language and literature can reflect,
convey, render, or refer to reality, and utterances do emanate
from a preexistent self, while according to the opposite view no
such connection to reality and self can be reached through language and literature. The approach I suggest replaces these two
relations by a third, which I call "access," whose different connotations allow mutually modifying insights from divergent positions. Access, as I see it, is no longer a relation between words and
things, but between different systems of signification, or different
signifying processes. In this, my view resembles the theories of
ideology mentioned above. Where it differs from them is in its
claim for more than misrepresentation or discursive, ideological
constructs. The approach I propose recognizes the problematic
status of the concepts of representation and subjectivity, and yet
attempts to save them from being both dismantled and totally en-
gulfed in discursive practices. I suggest that narration is the main
mode of access in literature (and perhaps life). On the one hand, it
destabilizes representation and subjectivity; on the other, it opens
a way to a modified and qualified rehabilitation.

Although representation and subjectivity can nourish many studies separately, and have often done so, I have decided to treat them together because they are two facets of the view of being as presence. *Presence,* the cornerstone of what has come to be called "logocentrism," designates both a world preceding expression and an "I" present to itself (see Derrida 1972, 193; 1976, 12). No wonder, then, that the same theoreticians who conceive of reality as preexisting language also see the "I" as resisting radical doubt, while theoreticians who question the existence of reality outside discourse also dismantle the autonomy of the individual. *Expressive realism* is the term Catherine Belsey uses to emphasize the affinity between representation and subjectivity in various trends of thinking. "Expressive realism," according to her, is "the theory that literature reflects the *reality* of experience as it is perceived by one (especially gifted) individual, who *expresses* it in a discourse which enables other individuals to recognize it as true" (1980, 7; Belsey's emphases). Belsey traces the transformations of this view from Aristotelian mimesis through the Renaissance, the eighteenth century, and Romanticism before proceeding to its undermining in what she calls the post-Saussurean perspective. The individual Belsey is concerned with is the author, but her description can be generalized to narrators and characters.

I conduct my exploration principally through an analysis of several twentieth-century novels that represent a theoretical avant-garde, a kind of laboratory where the problematics of representation and subjectivity is enacted, dramatized, and lived out, explicitly or implicitly, structurally and thematically. Literature has its own ways of "thinking" about conceptual problems, and theory can only benefit from integrating these alternative modes of knowing. Novelists manifest attitudes toward representation and subjectivity not by truth-claims or direct statements about correspondence to reality but by dramatizing relations among voices or positions.

I have chosen to analyze Faulkner's *Absalom, Absalom!* (1936), Nabokov's *The Real Life of Sebastian Knight* (1941),

Brooke-Rose's *Thru* (1975), Beckett's *Company* (1980), and Morrison's *Beloved* (1987)—all twentieth-century texts, because the issues I wish to examine have become particularly pressing in our period. The five novels share an interrogation of the problems of representation and subjectivity, though some put more emphasis on the former, others on the latter. They also dramatize these issues through an attempt to reproduce a personal and/or communal history. Narration plays a crucial role in the affinity that emerges between the problematics of reconstructing the past and retrieving memory and the problematics of representation and subjectivity.

The interaction between literary texts and conceptual problems outlines a twentieth-century movement from ambivalence about representation and subjectivity (*Absalom, Absalom!* and *The Real Life of Sebastian Knight*), to their negation or engulfment in discursive practices (*Thru;* partly in *Company*), to an attempt at regaining the lost possibilities (partly in *Company;* mainly in *Beloved*). The mapping of the moments punctuated by these novels is not new. What is new, I believe, and integral to the approach I advocate, is the analysis of the ways in which changing attitudes to representation and subjectivity are enacted by specific strategies of storytelling. In the novels I analyze, the problem of representation is dramatized mainly through a manipulation of narrative levels: their multiplication, analogies among them, and transgressions of the boundaries marking their separateness. The problem of subjectivity takes the form of undecidability concerning the narrator's identity and structural position vis-à-vis the events narrated. An explanation of some technical terms I use is given in the appendix.

The movement that emerges from my exploration of the novels is generally analogous to the transition from modernism to postmodernism to a countertendency within postmodernism. One must, however, remember that such transitions are never clear-cut; there is always a certain degree of overlap between trends. Modernism foregrounds epistemological problems, whereas postmodernism puts in doubt not only our capacity to know but also the ontological status of the world that is the object of knowledge (McHale 1987, 9–10). Many of the insights and techniques of both modernism and postmodernism have been incorporated by the countertendency I detect, but in it they have been used to re-engage with reality (hence also with representation) and rehumanize subjectivity. Though in no way exclusive to ethnic and feminist writing, reinstating inclinations are particularly strong in these literatures, which are motivated by the desire to rescue a history from the oblivion to which the majority group has consigned it and give a voice to those silenced by the system. From this perspective *Absalom, Absalom!* and *The Real Life of Sebastian Knight* can be seen as border texts between modernism and postmodernism, *Thru* as clearly postmodernist, *Company* as having one foot in mainstream postmodernism and one in the countertendency within it, and *Beloved* as a leading countertext within postmodernism. What is interesting, however, is not the labeling of the novels but the many parallels between the historical moments they stage, the larger literary movements, the conceptual trajectory of literary theory, and the shape of this exploration of theoretical issues through literature. Around these, encompassing them and rendering their affinity intelligible, are the contours of the cultural landscapes of our period.

1

Narration, Representation, Subjectivity

Once upon a time (or so some present-day theorists would like to believe), language was conceived of as imitating or mirroring reality. Whether anchored in interpretations of Aristotle's concept of mimesis or not,[1] such views assume a direct relation between words and things, between the verbal and the nonverbal domain. Words stand for something else; they become a transparent channel to an extralinguistic outside, which is taken to exist before its verbalization. An awareness of the nontransparency of language and of its problematic relation to the world has often led to the replacement of *mimesis* by *representation* and of *reality* by *reality-models, schemata,* or any number of related terms. While denying language the capacity to imitate a nonlinguistic reality, many traditional views of representation still conceive of language and literature as articulations, reproductions of a prior presence.[2] No wonder, then, that *representation* in this sense is often conflated with *mimesis,* as in Auerbach's seminal study (1953) or in the widespread use of the adjectives *mimetic* and *nonmimetic* in debates about representation. Traces of the tradition can be detected even within narratology, which has often aligned itself with a nonhumanist ideology. The logical priority of reality (or, in more cautious formulations, fictional reality) underlies formalist and structuralist conceptions of *fabula* and *histoire,* whether these are explicitly seen as preceding the *sjužet* or *récit,* or as abstracted and reconstructed from it. Similarly, if one defines narration as a verbal act "consisting of someone telling someone else that something happened" (Smith 1980, 232), one grants the events a logical priority over their telling.[3]

The difference between the notion of mimesis and traditional concepts of representation hinges on the nature of the relation between language and reality (imitation versus reference, correspondence, adequation, standing for). Neither the existence of *some* relation nor the antecedence of reality is questioned. But the radicalization of the critique in post-Saussurean linguistics, in the philosophies of Heidegger, Wittgenstein, Derrida, and their adherents, and in Lacanian psychoanalysis has given rise to the dichotomy that I will here simplify as the possibility versus the impossibility of representation. Grave doubts have been cast on the capacity of language to reach—let alone represent—the world. The presumption of the existence of a reality prior to the act of representation has also come under fire. Some see the world as "always already textualized by an arche-writing or system of differentiation," and as "a mirage of language," to be excluded from linguistic and literary discussion (Scholes 1980, 206). Instead of a thing-in-itself, reality is now considered an absence, and language replaces, rather than reflecting or even conveying, this absent reality.

Let me linger a little on the case of psychoanalysis, because narration is of paramount importance in it, and the development of my own view must therefore take careful account of the destabilization of representation from this perspective. Psychoanalysis believes that the traumatic experiences that influence a person's whole life tend to be repressed, that is, made absent to consciousness. These "absent" events, experiences that are not remembered, get repeated and acted out in the person's life and in the process of transference (see, e.g., Freud 1958). Since, as far as consciousness goes, the repressed is an absence for the analysand, its repetition becomes in a sense the first presence, the first "performance" of the absence. Going beyond the notion of the repressed experiences as an absence to consciousness, Lacan claims that they are also absent in the sense of never having occurred in the person's life. According to Lacan, "It is less out of anything real . . . than precisely out of *what never was,* that what repeats itself springs" (translated in Johnson 1978, 504). If Freud is right in maintaining that most infantile repressions have to do with the Oedipus complex, the castration complex, and their ramifications, then these would seem to represent events that have not occurred. A male child, the argument goes, has not been castrated by his father for his desire to sleep with his mother; he has only interpreted the absence of a penis in the female as a castration which threatens him. Barbara Johnson's conclusion is that

> Psychoanalysis is in fact *itself* the primal scene it is seeking: it is the *first* occurrence of what has been repeating itself in the patient without ever having occurred. Psychoanalysis is not itself the *interpretation* of repetition; it is the repetition of a *trauma of interpretation* called "castration" or "parental coitus" or "the Oedipus complex" or even "sexuality"—the traumatic deferred interpretation not *of* an event but *as* an event which never took place as such. The "primal scene" is not a scene but an *interpretative infelicity* whose result was to situate the interpreter in an intolerable position. And psychoanalysis is the reconstruction of that interpretative infelicity not as *its* interpretation, but as its first and last *act*. Psychoanalysis has content only insofar as it repeats the dis-content of what never took place. (1978, 499; Johnson's emphases)

One may wish to take issue with these views both as interpretations of Freud's theories and in themselves, for example, by querying the equivalence they establish between absence to consciousness (epistemological absence) and absence *tout court* (ontological absence). True, the repressed is absent to consciousness, but—at least in Freud—it is present in the unconscious. No less problematic is the radical form of absence discussed by Lacan and Johnson. Most male children have not been castrated by their fathers, nor have they slept with their mothers (although we know now that incest is much more widespread than was thought in the past), but if, as psychoanalysis claims, they have fantasized such a scenario, hasn't there been a psychic event? And can one really speak of absence except metaphorically? Moreover, the psychic event, which Johnson would call an interpretation, is often (though not always) based on an actual event—the child's overhearing the "cries and whispers" of his or her parents while making love. My purpose here is not to argue with the centrality of absence in Lacanian psychoanalysis but rather to anticipate a relationship that will be useful in developing my own approach later.

Just as the critique of mimesis has led to the alternative notion of representation, so has the interrogation of representation given rise to new alternatives. But while substituting *representation* for *mimesis* was a modification, the alternatives to representation, particularly creation, play, textuality, intertextuality, and metatextuality, present themselves as counterconcepts.

If the literary situation, like its psychoanalytic counterpart, is a performative repetition of an absence, then representation gives way to presentation, reproduction to production, and re-creation to creation. Spariosu relates such views to the "romantic ideology which privileged the subject as constituting rather than 'imitating' or 'reflecting' the object" (1982, 53). He also relates it to the Einsteinian revolution in physics, where the claim is no longer "to disclose a certain (objective) reality, but rather to *invent* it" (ibid., 33). Whereas Descartes, speaking of the properties of triangles, stated, "No one can say that I have invented or imagined them," mathematicians today say precisely this. In *The Evolution of Physics*, Einstein talks constantly about the "important invention" of the electromagnetic field and all the other realities "created by modern physics," and he rejoices in the new concepts because they have enabled us "to create a more subtle reality" (quoted in Spariosu 1982, 33). Similarly, for Feyerabend, "Facts do not create the theory, but theory creates its own facts" (ibid.).

From this perspective, language and literature are seen as a creation rather than a re-creation of reality. Creation in this sense is closely related to the concept of play, which has become a catchword since Derrida, but which is equally central to the recent theorizing of a non-deconstructionist like Wolfgang Iser. In "The Play of the Text," Iser says: "The following essay is an attempt to raise play above representation as an umbrella concept to cover all the ongoing operations of the textual process. It has two heuristic advantages: (1) play does not have to concern itself with what it might stand for, and (2) play does not have to picture anything outside itself. It allows author-text-reader to be conceived as a dynamic interrelationship that moves toward a final result" (1989, 250). The connection between play, creation, and absence becomes clear later in the essay: "The play-movement takes place when the schema ceases to function as a form of accommodation, and instead of taking its shape from the object to be imitated, now imposes a shape on what is absent" (1989, 254–55).

The concept of play, especially in its variant as the "free play of signifiers," does not always lead to a view of literature as creating, rather than re-creating, a reality. Indeed, reality, whether re-created or created, is often completely excluded from nonrepresentational approaches, and what literature is said to produce is pure textuality. If, within the representational framework, writing and narrating are seen as transitive verbs (they tell something), according to the opposite view both become intransitive verbs: They tell, or even better, they merely unfold (Barthes 1972).

Like textuality, intertextuality is frequently opposed to representation. Whereas representation is based on a reference from words to things, intertextuality is a reference from words to words, or rather from texts to texts. The concept of "text" is often expanded to designate the whole world. The world, as a network of signs, becomes a text (or series of texts); intertextuality replaces representation.

As an alternative to representation, metatextuality can be added to textuality and intertextuality. The despair that arises from confronting the incapacity of language to "reach" the world is sometimes counteracted by a search for a metalinguistic place from which to speak of the limitations of language and literature (Thiher 1984, 117). This results in metatexts, self-conscious or self-referential literature, works that interrogate or dramatize their own difficulties in representing reality. Such works often function as a kind of metacommentary on theory or philosophy, discourses that more commonly enjoy a metastatus in relation to literature.

An inalienable essence, uniqueness (or individuality), unity, and stability (or continuity)—these are the most common attributes of the self in its traditional conceptions, and they have all been challenged by novelists and theoreticians in our century. Frequently, the self is seen as a contingency of roles and functions (Mead 1934). The notion of individuality or uniqueness gives place to that of an anonymous, prehuman stratum underlying all singular variations (Lawrence 1914; Sarraute 1956). Unity has been replaced by "the divided self" (Laing 1960), "the split subject" (Lacan 1966), "a group acting together" (Cixous 1974). And stability gives way to flux (Woolf 1925). "The researches of psychoanalysis, of linguistics, of anthropology," writes Foucault, "have 'decentered' the subject in relation to the laws of its desire, the forms of its language, the rules of its actions, or the play of its mythical and imaginative discourse" (1969, 22). The verb *decenter,* it is worth noting, is used here, as in many contemporary writings, in two different, though perhaps related, senses. One has to do with the absence or loss of an inner center holding together the different aspects of the individual. The other concerns the replacement of the anthropocentric view by an outlook that puts impersonal systems rather than people in the center. To use Culler's description, "The self is dissolved as its various functions are ascribed to impersonal systems which operate through it" (1981, 33).[4]

A corollary of both senses of decentering is observable in the language used by Foucault, namely the substitution of the term *subject* for *self.* Like the grammatical subject, the human subject is reduced in this theory to a structural position in a system governed by differences. Similarly, in Lacan's linguistically based psychoanalysis, *subject* refers to the *individual* when s/he is inserted into the symbolic order, i.e., the order of language, law, social systems, "the name of the father"—systems of differences in which the subject undergoes an alienation from him/herself and is subjected to signifying chains.

As is well known, the dissolution of the self has had devastating consequences for the status of characters in narrative fiction as well as for the author's mode of existence (or nonexistence) within the text. Since I foreground narration, my focus is on the relations between the teller and his/her utterances. Reformulated from this limited perspective, the traditional view holds that utterances presuppose, or constitute, a stance from which they are conducted, and that this stance is attributable to a voice emanating from a self. The more recent views, on the other hand, contend that the public system of language, its rule-governed character, the play of rhetorical devices and intertextual references, and the presence of aporias and internal splits are signs of a disconnection between language and an individual voice and self (see Harrison 1991, 188–218). The speaker is considered "a storehouse of his culture's linguistic system, of its codes, syntagms, and potential paradigmatic options" (Thiher 1984, 128). Voice becomes a position within the linguistic system, and the knowable self a linguistic construct (a subject). Heidegger's famous statement "Die Sprache spricht! nicht der Mensch" is by now almost a truism, reverberating in Wittgenstein's tenet that play is not defined by people but rather defines them, as well as by the deconstructionist idea that we are spoken by language, and Barthes's declaration: "Le discours, ou mieux encore, le langage parle, c'est tout" (1970, 48).

In narratology proper, the divergence of opinion focuses mainly on the narrator's mode of existence. Classically, the narrator corresponded to a fictional person whose psychological makeup and moral values could be reconstructed from the text, even when the narrator is omniscient, a voice external to the narrated events (see, e.g., Booth 1961; Ewen 1974). In structuralist narratology, on the other hand, the narrator is often treated as a narrative *instance,* and if the term *voice* is used (Genette 1972; Rimmon-Kenan 1983), it is taken in a quasi-grammatical sense, restricted to the narrator's structural position with regard to the narrated world. This is consistent with the narratological depersonification of the traditionally personlike agents in narrative fiction, namely, the exclusion of the author and the implied author and the reduction of characters to the sum total of their actions. In deconstruction, the very notion of a narrator becomes superfluous. The text is performed by language, not by a specific person, voice, or even *instance.*

The conflicting views concerning both representation and subjectivity are refined yet duplicated by the largely deconstructionist insights that differences exist not only between positions but also within them, and that opposites, being each other's polar condition of possibility, generate each other in perpetual oscillation. In the process of deconstructing the possibility of representation as well as of literal meaning, de Man inserts a significant caveat: "It would be quite foolish to assume that one can lightheartedly move away from the constraint of referential meaning" (1979, 201). In typical zigzag fashion, however, he follows this with a claim that in Rousseau's *Second Discourse,* referential language "becomes an aberrant trope that conceals the radical figurality of language behind the illusion that it can properly mean" (ibid., 202). At the far end of de Man's deconstruction of the self there is a recuperation of this very notion, but the retrieval uncannily includes its own negation:

> In all these instances, rhetoric functions as a key to the discovery of the self, and it functions with such ease that one may well begin to wonder whether the lock indeed shapes the key or whether it is not the other way round, that a lock (and a secret room or box behind it) had to be invented in order to give a function to the key. For what could be more distressing than a bunch of highly refined keys just lying around without any corresponding locks worthy of being opened? Perhaps there are none, and perhaps the most refined key of all, the key of keys, is the one that gives access to the Pandora's box in which this darkest secret is kept hidden. This would imply the existence of at least one lock worthy of being raped, the Self as the relentless undoer of selfhood. (ibid., 173)

What such complications show, I believe (and the insight goes beyond the specific concepts of representation and subjectivity) is that any two propositions, considered as totalities in a binary opposition, inevitably generate each other, become a necessary other for each other. "The pressure toward meaning and the pressure toward its undoing can never cancel each other out" (de Man 1979, 161), and even the most powerful critiques of logocentrism cannot escape the logocentric premises they undermine. Prendergast describes this interdependence in terms of the liar's paradox: "It places logical constraints upon the attack on mimesis and representational discourse generally, in that any such attack is obliged, as a condition of its intelligibility, to adopt the very categories of the object it attacks." This predicament can easily be seen in Derrida's work: "Derrida's own deconstruction of the set of terms which support the mimetic project (truth, reference, etc.) is—self-confessedly—impossible without recourse to these terms" (Prendergast 1986, 18).

Within the deconstructionist framework, any (hypothetical) impulse to transcend dichotomies would automatically engender the undercutting recognition that dichotomies cannot be transcended, and this new pair of opposites would start a further movement of oscillation, and so on and on in ever-increasing self-consciousness. Such a movement comes to a halt (or perhaps never begins) in theories of ideology inspired by Althusser and Foucault. Here the question whether representation is or is not possible is literally im-pertinent, because representation is, from the start, dissociated from reality. In these views, which permeate some versions of semiotics, feminism, New Historicism, and British cultural materialism, representation is related not to reality but to discursive practices. The practices are ideological constructs, and the term *ideology* designates "not the system of the real relations which govern the existence of individuals, but the imaginary relation of those individuals to the real relations in which they 'live'" (Althusser 1971, 165). Ideology, in this sense, functions as unproclaimed fiction, wool over one's eyes, in the service of the powers that be. As a discursive, ideological construct, representation becomes re-presentation, that is, presenting again and again: "Ideology is always repeated, always re-presented, always already 'known' from previous discourses, images and myths. Ideology re-presents not the real, nor a distorted reflection of the real, but the 'obvious.' What it suppresses is its own construction in signifying practice" (Belsey 1980, 148 n. 10). Within this conceptual framework, subjectivity is a type of representation, linguistically and discursively constructed, informed by ideology, and having no unmediated relation to an experience of self and others.

Given a conception of representation as that which is constructed in and by discourse (or by some other signifying system), having no connection to the world, the whole question of the capacity or incapacity of language and literature to represent reality becomes irrelevant. This does not mean, however, as some deconstructionist writing holds, that representation is impossible. On the contrary, representation is everywhere, but its meaning is completely changed. Such studies regularly shift from the singular to the plural, from "representation" to "representations."[5] This move is motivated partly by an insistence on the plurality of coexisting discourses and partly by the use of *representation* to designate not the act or process of representing but its products, represented objects. These theories of ideology collapse not only the possible/impossible dichotomy but also the presumed contrast between representation and its counterconcepts. An example: Earlier in this chapter, the view of language and literature as constructing (creating) reality was presented as opposed to its view as reconstructing (representing) it. Here they are treated as quasi-synonymous. Below is part of a statement from a semiotic feminist study influenced by these new directions, where the quasi-synonymity is implied by the parallelism of the appositive clauses: "If we then want to bring our bodies and our pleasures closer, where we might see what they are like; better still, where we might *represent* them from another perspective, *construct* them with another standard of measurement, or understand them within other terms of analysis" (de Lauretis 1987, 38; emphases mine). Representation becomes paradoxically contained within the view that questioned it, a form of construction, rather than its binary opposite. I have no desire to ignore the destabilization of representation or its alignment with construction. On the contrary, I wish to integrate these views in my rethinking. But I feel uncomfortable with the complete divorce between representation and reality, between subjectivity and selves.

Nor is my discomfort idiosyncratic. Quite a few moral philosophers today return to the notion of self (e.g., Taylor 1989;

Harrison 1991) and reinject human agency into theories that had
emphasized the dominance of social systems and ideological constructs.[6] Moreover, realignments with reality and selves are often
mediated by the notion of narrative. Alisdair MacIntyre thus
speaks about "the narrative unity of life" (1981); Paul Ricoeur in-
vokes the "narrative identity which constitutes us" (1991).
Ricoeur's view is most relevant here because it uses narrative to
reflect about both representation and subjectivity, and it explicitly relates to narratological models like Genette's.

Rejecting the neat opposition between stories and reality, as it
expresses itself, for example, in the dictum, "Stories are recounted
and not lived; life is lived and not recounted," Ricoeur insists on a
multiplicity of arguments, which "compel us to grant to experience as such a virtual narrativity" (1991, 29). To him, lived experience is a chain of stories that demand to be told, and—like
reality—the subject also emerges from potential stories in which
he or she is entangled. The advantage of the concept of narrative
identity, according to Ricoeur, is that it replaces the view of identity as sameness (*idem*) by that of identity as self (*ipse*), giving
room for change, development, dynamism.

These are attractive views, and so is their development in
Ricoeur's *Time and Narrative* (1985). But Ricoeur foregrounds
narrative, the product, whereas I emphasize narration, the process of production. This characterization of Ricoeur's endeavor
may sound inaccurate, since he takes narratology to task for ne-
glecting narration and confining analysis only to its traces in the
accomplished narrative: "Narratology, however, strives to record
only the marks of narration found in the text" (1985, 82). Closer
scrutiny, however, reveals that Ricoeur's concern with narration
(or narrating) is limited to its temporality. In criticizing Genette,
he says: "Postponing any discussion of the time of narration is
not without its drawbacks" (85), and later: "These pages [of
Genette's] are at the very least premature, when we consider that
the study of the time of narration is postponed" (86). But narra-

tion, as I see it, is an ongoing process, constantly open to what T. S. Eliot calls "visions and revisions," offering a glance toward the concepts under consideration rather than freezing them as stable, secure products. Another advantage of my emphasis on narration is the hierarchy it both establishes and disrupts between narrative levels.

Enter narration, and it enters as a mode of access. By *narration,* I mean the act or process of telling—whether by an external narrating voice, by an internal character-narrator, or by a character within the narrative who tells a story within the overall story. Behind all these is the author's act of narration, which (as I argue in the conclusion) calls for a reexploration in a separate study. Here I will consider the author only when his/her role is foregrounded by the text under consideration. I use the term *access* here because its connotations are double-edged. This term's duality epitomizes an argument that both incorporates the problematization of representation and subjectivity and reestablishes them in spite of doubt. In playing with the various connotations of *access,* I am consciously engaged in a game not very different from the one practiced by Shreve and Quentin in *Absalom, Absalom!* By letting metaphor, analogy, and *mise en abyme* function as arguments, I wish to emphasize my position about literature's way of "knowing" and the advantages of theorizing through literature.

This said, "let me play a while now" (*Absalom, Absalom!* 280). On the one hand, *access* means "approach," "passage," "channel," "doorway," implying the presence of some further space. By analogy, this suggests that narration opens or constitutes a direct approach to reality and subjectivity. On the other hand, "Access" has also become the brand name of one kind of credit card. A credit card is granted purchasing power because— on the basis of trust inscribed in institutionalized conventions—it represents a promise of money (even if the money is not available in the user's bank account at that moment). Money, of course, is a sign system, a representation, and a credit card is thus a representation of a representation. The operative relation here is not between signs and things but between two sign systems. In fact, the situation is even more complex. Money does not directly represent the object to be purchased; it signifies what economists call "value." Value is measured in relation to other values, leading to a layering of differential systems. These systems give access to things in the world on the basis of an act of substitution that again involves a convention-governed trust or faith.

Like the use of a credit card, the act of narration does not represent the world directly. Rather, it represents modes of representation, possibilities of doubt and credence, in the worlds the characters inhabit. These may be filtered through a variety of narrators and points of view or through other forms of what Bakhtin (1981) calls "polyphony" and "heteroglossia." From the point of view of ideological theories, narration can be seen as putting in motion an interaction between discursive practices, but—as in the credit card analogy—I believe that the interaction issues in a gesture of substitution offering indirect access to a "world." The whole process, and in particular the final leap, requires—like the operation of "Access"—trust or faith governed by convention.

The idea of access (without the credit card association) has become accessible to me through both Jameson and Iser, although Jameson talks about historiography and Iser (like myself) about fiction,[7] Jameson emphasizes the "represented reality," while Iser deals with the "representing appearance," and their positions on the issues in question are far from similar. Resisting the deconstructionist dismantling of reality in historiography, Jameson says:

> What Althusser's own insistence on history as an absent cause makes clear, but what is missing from the formula as it is canonically worded, is that he does not at all draw the fashionable conclusion that because history is a text, the "referent"

does not exist. We would therefore propose the following revised formulation: that history is *not* a text, not a narrative, master or otherwise, but that, as an absent cause, it is inaccessible to us except in textual form, and that approach to it and to the Real itself necessarily passes through its prior textualization, its narrativization in the political unconscious. (1980, 35)

True, Jameson speaks about "narrativization" (presumably meaning organization as a narrative), not about "narration" (the act or process of telling), but his narrativization, like my narration, is seen as the only access to what is otherwise inaccessible. The status of history in Jameson's theory is complex. It is an "absent cause," yet by no means a nonexistent referent; it is "the Real," but the Real in a Lacanian sense, hence also "the Impossible." Jameson both affirms and undercuts reality in this paradoxical statement; he problematizes and insists on representation.

Iser's stance, on the other hand, is explicitly antirepresentational, although on close scrutiny his "mode of access" may invite a reading against the grain. Every appearance, says Iser, "is a faked mode of access to what cannot become present" (1993, 300), and "staging prevents the inaccessible from being occupied. It does give form to the inaccessible but it preserves the status of the latter by revealing itself as a simulacrum" (ibid., 301). "Faked or unfaked" is a matter of truth-value; access and giving form belong to the operative realm. By putting the emphasis on mode of access rather than on faked, Iser's statement can be read as (or turned into?) an affirmation of *some* contact in spite of the problematic nature of the mode and the inaccessibility of the object.

So much for representation. How does the Access analogy operate for subjectivity? A credit card is operative in a given system only on the basis of a number specific to its owner. The number, itself a sign, does not express the essence of its owner; it only represents the subject by differentiating him/her from other subjects.

Like the personal number on a credit card, the narrating subject is at least "something that might make a mark on something," to use *Absalom, Absalom!* again (127). In addition, a circularity governs both "Access" and narration. Just as a credit card simultaneously assumes a user and inscribes him/her as a personal number, so narration both presupposes a narrator and creates him/her in the process of telling.

An approach through narration also grants the narrating subject access to agency within (or in spite of) the ideological constructs to which he or she is subjected. Since, as Bakhtin and others have shown, there are several competing discourses at any given time, one form of (fairly limited) freedom is the ability to choose a specific discourse in which to take up a position.[8] It is not my purpose here to offer a list of the possibly infinite ways in which narrators can position themselves within discourses. Some will come up in the textual analyses that follow (chapters 2 through 6 below). For the sake of clarity, however, let me draw again on *Absalom, Absalom!*—the novel from which all the brief examples in this section are taken—to illustrate one type of self-positioning. Here the character-narrators invest their discourse with certain generic characteristics informed by their chosen attitude toward the events threatening to imprison them. Rosa's narrative is imbued with a Gothic spirit, Mr. Compson's with the spirit of Greek tragedy, Quentin narrates a chivalric romance, and Shreve ironically spins a tall tale. Of course, the generic characteristics are also discursive constructs, inscribing subjects within themselves, but in these instances the inscriptions are self-willed, a mark of the narrating subject. Going beyond such a mark of the narrating subject, Bakhtin grants him/her "an internally persuasive discourse," achieved by interweaving "others' words" and "one's own word" (1981, 342–46). "One's own word" is, of course, not ideology-free, but it does permit "play with its borders" and "spontaneously creative stylizing variants" (343)—a certain degree of freedom.[9]

From a different perspective, the very structure of the relation between the act of narration and the narrated events potentially frees the narrating subject from complete unconscious entrapment in discursive practices. According to Althusser, the subject believes him/herself to be outside ideology, although in fact s/he is totally in it. I suggest that this need not apply to the narrating subject because of the doubleness of his/her position.[10] The classical model, as it has come to us from Genette (1972), conceives of the act or process responsible for producing the narrative as being, by definition, on a higher logical level than the story it narrates. By the same token, narration within a narrative is above the events it tells, this being the governing principle of Genette's distinction between narrative levels (see the appendix for explanation). The same applies to so-called first-person narratives, where the narrator as a speaking subject is at a higher level than his/her (usually younger) version as a protagonist. This logical position of narration as against a narrated "reality" allows it to maintain a certain freedom from the network of illusions in which—according to ideological theories—it is enmeshed qua discursive practice. The narrator in the classical model is positioned not only in the hierarchy of levels but also in a lateral relation of participation, the difference here being between inside and outside (a narrator who is or is not part of the narrated events). The very possibility of being outside, of telling the story of another, creates a certain distance; but even when the narrator is part of the narrated "reality," perhaps even its protagonist, complete unconscious entrapment may be inhibited by the split in the hierarchy between protagonist and narrator.

That there can be a stance above or outside ideological constructs is precisely what theories of ideology question, along with the narratological model that makes room for it. Am I not, then, involved in a circular argument? Yes and no. The hierarchy of levels and lateral relations that, to my mind, secures a certain degree of distance or freedom on the part of the narrating subject is seen by various ideological theorists as a subordination of other voices to the narrator's "higher authority" (Seltzer 1984; Bender 1987; Miller 1988). My own position is the reverse: There would be no narrative levels and no lateral relations without a proliferation of different versions and disparate understandings of the events, often complicating those of the overall narrator. Each voice has a certain degree of freedom in relation to the events it narrates, and ideology in the novel (I agree with Bakhtin) cannot totalize and unify all subject-positions. The novels discussed below also problematize the classical model in different degrees through a multiplication of narrative levels and a creation of analogies and metalepses among them, as well as by an undecidability concerning the identity of the narrator and his/her position with regard to the narrated objects.[11] However, the novels also suggest (in varying degrees) a return to representation and subjectivity through a different use of the same destabilizing strategies. Thus, for example, the construction of the subject sometimes depends on a detour via the other (which involves blurring the inside/outside distinction), and the multiplication of narrative levels (hence also of narrators) can become a way of taking charge of one's own subjectivity as well as of gaining a convoluted and indirect access to a "reality." This doubleness explains why my exploration of representation and subjectivity through five transitional twentieth-century novels has come to focus on narrative levels and the identity of the narrator.

For an exploration by means of literature, however, the discussion has remained abstract for too long. Let me now move toward concreteness by surveying the ways in which the novels "theorize" representation and subjectivity through strategies of narration. Faulkner's *Absalom, Absalom!* and Nabokov's *The Real Life of Sebastian Knight* are, in different ways, under the sign of conflict. In *Absalom, Absalom!* the belief in representation is juxtaposed with the playfulness of creation. The narrators' reliability, as well as the status of narration as a reconstruction of (past) reality, is undermined by the multiplication of narrative levels, the absence or slanting of first-hand narration, each narrator's telling mainly what he or she has heard from others, and the contradictions among the narrators. All these obstacles to reliability in the classical sense become assets when one conceives of narration as invention or imaginative creation. This conception ripples inward to the level of the events and outward to the reading process, and in all cases creation is seen not only as a manifestation of free play but also as an exercise of power.

The problematic status of subjectivity is dramatized in this novel by two main features of narration. Whereas the direct participants in the drama (with the exception of Rosa) do not narrate, those who do narrate did not participate in the events. As a result, the subjectivity of the non-narrating characters is, to a large extent, a construction by others: You are what others say about you. Conversely, the narrating characters become subjects by telling about others, or rather "living," enacting the objects of their narration: You are what you say (performatively) about others. Further complications arise from difficulties in attributing utterances to speakers, caused by a frequent ambiguity or indeterminacy of the speaker, a superimposition of voices, and a uniformity of style. I will discuss narratological, thematic, and deconstructive "solutions," the first two seen as enhancing the connection between narration and originating subject, the last as challenging it.

In Nabokov's *The Real Life of Sebastian Knight,* the problem of representation is filtered through the attempt to reconstruct a "real life" of an individual. I therefore start my analysis by focusing on the destabilization of the roles of narrating subject and narrated object. Is the novel a biography, V telling Sebastian's story? Or is it an autobiography, Sebastian telling his own story, using V as a persona? Further complications arise from the autobiography hypothesis, for the novel might also be V's (intended or unintended) narration of his own life-story through Sebastian. By blocking the choice between these alternatives, the novel suggests both the alienation of the subject through the other and the constitution of the other through the narrating subject.

Like *Absalom, Absalom!, The Real Life of Sebastian Knight* oscillates between affirming the possibility of representation and dismantling it by showing how reality recedes before layers of narration and by putting in doubt the reliability of all the narrators. The act of telling, which is unable to reach reality, becomes a struggle over the power to shape it by shaping the narrative. The conflict between representation and creation acquires an additional dimension in *The Real Life of Sebastian Knight,* as creation takes the self-reflexive form of the writing of fiction. Analogies and metalepses between narrative levels manifest the interchangeability between reality and fiction. The analogies between Sebastian's novels and Sebastian's life reinforce the representational view of narration, the novels being conceived as rendering the life. On the other hand, the analogies and metalepses between Sebastian's novels and V's quest reveal the former as dictating the latter, and by implication fiction as creating reality. By foregrounding the fictionality of reality and the reality of fiction, as well as destabilizing not only the concept of representation but also that of reality, *The Real Life of Sebastian Knight* becomes a more radical questioning of representation than *Absalom, Absalom!* though it too does not abandon representation completely.

Whereas *Absalom, Absalom!* and *The Real Life of Sebastian Knight* are conflicted (in different degrees) about representation and subjectivity, Brooke-Rose's *Thru* comes very close to a total deconstruction of both. More extreme than any analogies and metalepses is the book's reversibility of the hierarchy usually assumed to exist among narrative levels. Like Escher's famous *Drawing Hands, Thru* playfully frustrates any attempt to distinguish between narrating subject and narrated object, container and contained, outside and inside, higher and lower narrative levels. It plunges the reader into a universe of paradox, infinite regress, and tight loop, collapsing the presumed separation between reality and narration and subverting the very notion of representation. The subverted notion gives way to creation, play, textuality, intertextuality, and metatextuality. However, since *Thru* sees the whole world as a text, the textuality of literature becomes a dramatization of the textuality of the world, so that the novel has an unexpected representational dimension. Representation of a more traditional type is also present in *Thru,* especially where love and sex, gender inequality, illness, and various ideologies are concerned. Yet these themes tend to undergo a deconstruction soon after being scenically rendered. They are also often revealed as constructs within "delirious discourses," social clichés through which subjects "live" their own experiences.

Intertwined with the dismantling of representation is the dissolution of the traditional self. By turning narrating subjects into narrated (or invented) objects, reversing narrative levels depersonifies narrators, and they become texts, stories, even fictions. The confusion of voices, the quick and often unmarked transition from one narrator to another, and the abundant use of intertextuality all contribute to the effacement of any link between narration and an autonomous self. The narrator as an originating self dies in the act or process of narration, even as the process gives birth to a speaking subject who is a signifier in the symbolic order, endowed by ideological discourse with the illusory status of a self.

Beckett's *Company* has many affinities with *Thru,* but it also offers a tentative access to the dismantled concepts on a different plane. As in *Thru,* representation is subverted by a reversibility of the hierarchy between narrators and objects of narration. Yet while *Thru* prevents narration from being associated with any originating consciousness, *Company* finally does come to rest within the mind of the one on his back in the dark. This devising mind becomes the object of representation, and—from this point of view—the reversibility of narrative levels enacts different positions of the mind in relation to itself: The mind talks to itself about itself, occasionally perceives itself as if from the outside, and often imagines—or even invents—its own activity.

Equally double-edged is the treatment of the subject. One can see the splitting of narration into sections in the second person and sections in the third, as well as the explicit avoidance of the first person, as a dramatization of the dissolution of the traditional self. The severing of the present from the past, the focus on separate parts of the body rather than the whole, and the fragmentation of the text parallel the self's dissolution. These symptoms may also indicate the self-alienation that language necessitates. The limitations of language are often considered responsible for the reduction of the traditional self to a subject (or better, several subjects) in *Company*. But what is a reduction from one perspective becomes a celebration of plurality and freedom from another—the freedom of a plural subject from rigidifying conceptualizations in both language and philosophy. And the other side of fragmentation is reduplication, an emergence of otherness, which is a necessary condition for both company and narration.

Morrison's *Beloved* is no less obsessed with narratives and narration than the four novels discussed above, nor is it oblivious to the problems of representation and subjectivity. Nevertheless, it becomes—even more strongly than *Company*—a complex rehabilitation of these concepts through narration. The conditions necessary for acceding to what the novel calls "a self" emerge from a comparison between the multilayered telling of Denver's birth, rendered as memories of stories, and the primary narration of Beloved's second coming, or rebirth. In Denver's case, the layering of focalization and narration is necessary: only through memory and storytelling is birth transformed into a claim of ownership and an access to self. Beloved's rebirth, however, is not rendered through her memories (as focalizer) or her retrospective telling (as narrator), since these would have constituted her "self," which is precisely what Beloved does not have. Objective correlatives of this lack are Beloved's physical fragmentation and her incapacity to dissociate herself from Sethe. The multiplication of narrative levels, which in the earlier texts enacted a doubt about the possibility of reaching reality and constituting a self, operates in *Beloved* as an access to both.

Similarly, ambiguity, the Fantastic, and magical realism— techniques often used for nonrepresentational, self-reflexive pur- poses—are subordinate in *Beloved* to the attempt (and the difficulty) of making believable the unbelievable horrors of sla- very, of trying to represent an unbearable reality. The ambiguity of Beloved's mode of existence (natural/supernatural) enacts the tension inherent in such an enterprise as well as the double-edged response to trauma.

Culminating in a glimpse of retrieval, the path sketched in the preceding overview is fairly optimistic. Nevertheless, I do not wish to project the "glance beyond doubt" back onto texts where conflicts or skepticism predominate, for that would be an anach- ronism unworthy of both the literary texts and the historico-theo- retical trajectory I am trying to trace. Maintaining a delicate balance between the overall approach—derived mainly from within the novels—and the intricacies of narration in each text is one of the challenges of the specific analyses that follow.

2

William Faulkner, *Absalom, Absalom!*

"Something is always missing"

In the process of telling the Sutpen saga to his son, Quentin, Mr. Compson pauses to meditate on the limitations of his narration:

> It's just incredible. It just does not explain. Or perhaps that's it: they don't explain and we are not supposed to know. We have a few old mouth-to-mouth tales; we exhume from old trunks and boxes and drawers letters without salutation or signature, in which men and women who once lived and breathed are now merely initials or nicknames out of some now incomprehensible affection which sound to us like Sanskrit or Chocktaw; we see dimly people, the people in whose living blood and seed we ourselves lay dormant and waiting, in this shadowy attenuation of time possessing now heroic proportions, performing their acts of simple passion and simple violence impervious to time and inexplicable—Yes, Judith, Bon, Henry, Sutpen: all of them. They are there, yet something is missing; they are like a chemical formula ex-

humed along with the letters from that forgotten chest, carefully, the paper old and faded, almost indecipherable, yet
meaningful, familiar in shape and sense, the name and presence of volatile and sentient forces; you bring them together in
the proportions called for, but nothing happens; you re-read,
tedious and intent, poring, making sure that you have forgotten nothing, made no miscalculation; you bring them together
again and again nothing happens: just the words, the symbols,
the shapes themselves, shadowy inscrutable and serene,
against the turgid background of a horrible and bloody
mischancing of human affairs. (100–101)[1]

Narration, conceived by Mr. Compson as a reconstruction of past
events, is frustrated by the intractability of facts. The pieces of information fail to form a complete puzzle, the fragments do not
cohere: "You bring them together in the proportions called for
but nothing happens." The letters—both Bon's literal letter to
Judith and "letter" as a metaphor for "the disappearance of natural presence" (Derrida 1976, 159), both epistles and characters of
the alphabet—are faded, illegible, as if written in a dead language. Moreover, they are "without salutation or signature," ef-
facing the signs of human existence on the part of both addresser
and addressee. What remains is "just the words, the symbols, the
shapes themselves, shadowy inscrutable and serene"—the materiality of the letter, the pure textuality of the text, one might be
tempted to say today. And yet Mr. Compson is not quite a
present-day deconstructionist. True, he can neither make sense of
reality nor reach the people who populated it, since something is
always missing. Nevertheless, reality, for him, is a presence, no
matter how dim the human perception of it may be: The writing is
"*almost* indecipherable, *yet meaningful*"; behind the words, there
was a "background of horrible and bloody mischancing of human affairs" and there *were* "men and women who once lived
and breathed." What exasperates Mr. Compson is the inaccessibility of reality, not its absence.

Compare this with the following characterization of the
Quentin-Shreve collaboration, and you glimpse in a nutshell the
novel's conflicting views of the relation between narration, representation, and subjectivity: "the two of them creating between
them, out of the rag-tag and bob-ends of old tales and talking,
people who perhaps had never existed at all anywhere, who,
shadows, were shadows not of flesh and blood which had lived
and died but shadows in turn of what were (to one of them at
least, to Shreve) shades too, quiet as the visible murmur of their
vaporizing breath" (303). Unlike Mr. Compson, Quentin and
Shreve do not attempt to reconstruct reality; they create it. And
instead of frustration with the evasiveness of facts, they delight
in their absence, for it gives them the freedom to invent: "Let
me play a while now" (280), says Shreve to Quentin. Appropriately, what they create is not shadows of "flesh and blood,"
but shadows of shades; not "men and women who once lived
and breathed," but "people who perhaps had never existed at all
anywhere."

These are explicit formulations of the conflicting positions that
inform the structure, the narrative strategies, and many of the
thematic concerns of *Absalom, Absalom!* The novel is a classic
case of the Chinese-box structure. Its outermost level is narrated
by an extradiegetic narrator who "reproduces" a series of narrative situations in which four intradiegetic narrators try their
hands at telling the elusive story. Chapter 1 is predominantly
Rosa's narration, chapters 2 through 4 predominantly Mr.
Compson's, and chapter 5 Rosa's again.[2] Quentin remains the
narratee in all these chapters. In the next three chapters the function of narrator alternates between Shreve and Quentin, and the
function of narratee alternates accordingly. Chapter 6 is predominantly Shreve's narration, chapter 7 Quentin's, and chapter 8
Shreve's once more. The last chapter is told by the extradiegetic narrator through a predominant focalization on Quentin's
consciousness.[3]

What do the various intradiegetic narrators relate? Most of the time they narrate what was previously told to them. Rosa tells partly what she herself experienced, partly what she heard from the townspeople ("she heard just what the town heard" [78]) and, indirectly and indistinctly, behind closed doors, from her father, her aunt, and her sister Ellen (e.g., 25, 27). Like her, Mr. Compson sometimes relies on rumors spread by the inhabitants of Jefferson ("That was all that the town was to know about him for a month" [32]; "and so the tale came through the negroes" [79]), sometimes reports what Ellen said ("it was Ellen who told this, with shrieks of amusement, more than once" [71]), and sometimes defers to Rosa's authority ("It (the wedding) was in the same Methodist church where he saw Ellen for the first time, according to Miss Rosa" [48]). But his main source of information is his father, General Compson, who in turn heard at least part of the story from Sutpen ("I have this from something your grandfather let drop one day and which he doubtless had from Sutpen himself in the same accidental fashion" [49]).

The number of intermediaries is even larger in the composite Quentin-Shreve narration, for Quentin tells Shreve partly what he heard from Rosa and partly what he heard from his father, who heard from General Compson, who heard from Sutpen. Shreve, in turn, has no other source of information than Quentin and repeats to Quentin what he has heard from him, which—we remember—is what Quentin heard from his father, Mr. Compson from his father, and General Compson from Sutpen. Signs that Shreve merely repeats to Quentin what the latter has told him abound in the text, for example: "'How was it?' Shreve said. 'You told me; how was it? you and your father shooting quail, the gray day after it had rained all night and the ditch the horses couldn't cross so you and your father got down and gave the reins to—what was his name? the nigger on the mule? Luster—Luster to lead them around the ditch'" (187). Or, acknowledging not only Quentin as source but also Quentin's own sources, Shreve says, "so your father said," "didn't your father say?" (320); "And yet this old gal, this aunt Rosa, told you that someone was hiding out there and you said it was Clytie or Jim Bond and she said No and so you went out there . . . and there was?" (216).[4]

What is the effect of the chain of narrators on the status of their narration? In classical Boothian terms, one could say that it creates a distance between the teller and the tale and casts a doubt on the reliability of the narrators, who often report what they do not know, sometimes also what their informants do not know. Rosa, for example, narrates with extreme vividness of concrete detail the scene of Sutpen fighting with his negroes in the presence of his own children. She even "reproduces" a dialogue between Ellen and Sutpen, thereby conferring an air of referentiality on the whole scene, and then adds, "But I was not there. I was not there to see the two Sutpen faces this time—once on Judith and once on the negro girl beside her—looking down through the loft" (30). In connection with the climactic murder scene, she says, "I heard an echo, but not the shot; I saw a closed door but did not enter it" (150).[5] Although she is often barred from direct contact with events, she insistently refuses to let "blank door[s]" (27) interfere with her "omnivorous and unrational hearing sense" (145): "Though even I could not have heard through the door at all, I could have repeated the conversation for them" (25).[6] How reliable is a piece of information gleaned from behind closed doors by a child of four? And how trustworthy is a reverberation of an echo? Rosa's other source of information, the townspeople, is no less problematic, since their attempts to accost Sutpen and "give him the opportunity to tell them who he was and where he came from and what he was up to" (34) invariably fail, and they too are reduced to "suspecting" (ibid.), "believing" (79), relying on "the cabin-to-cabin whispering of the negroes to spread the news" (106).

Aside from the climactic meeting with Henry, in which, as far as we can tell from the text, all that happens is a brief exchange of questions and answers repeating and mirroring each other, Quentin's knowledge is always indirect, wholly derived from his father and Rosa. Even more problematic is Shreve's narration, since he is further removed from the events, and when he tells things that Quentin has presumably never told him, we wonder where he got his information: "In fact, Quentin did not even tell Shreve what his father had said about the visit. Perhaps Quentin himself had not been listening when Mr. Compson related it that evening at home" (336).[7]

If Mr. Compson seems closer to the truth than the other narrators, we must remember that he too was absent from the events he narrates and that the reliability of his father's account is often hedged with doubt, because sometimes even General Compson has to rely on fallible sources: " . . . not your grandfather. He knew only what the town, the county, knew" (209). And even when he relies on Sutpen, the one storyteller who is not separated from experience by screens of other narrations, firm control over the facts is undermined, this time by Sutpen's failure of memory: "He didn't remember if it was weeks or months or a year they travelled" (224); "he did not remember just where nor when nor how his father had got it" (ibid.); "So he knew neither where he had come from nor where he was nor why" (227); nor did he remember "within a year on either side just how old he was" (ibid.). He may even have been in the dark about an important aspect of the crucial scene that gave birth to his design: "He didn't remember (or did not say) what the message was" (229). One begins to understand Shreve's amused impatience with Sutpen as a source of information: "You [Quentin] said he didn't remember how he got to Haiti, and then he didn't remember how he got into the house with the niggers surrounding it. Now you are going to tell me he didn't even remember getting married?" (225).

The possibility of unreliable knowledge on the part of the various narrators—inferred from their nonparticipation in the events they narrate, their reliance on other sources often removed from the experience narrated, and the failure of memory of the only source directly involved in the events—problematizes the status of narration as a representation or reconstruction of reality. This is aggravated by the four narrators' contradictions about some of the basic occurrences. The principal contradictions are between Shreve and Quentin, on the one hand, and Rosa and Mr. Compson, on the other. Whereas Mr. Compson elaborates on Henry's puritan shock at seeing the octoroon (108–18), Shreve and Quentin believe that both she and her child "would have been to Henry only something else about Bon to be, not envied but aped if that had been possible" (336). Shreve also argues with Mr. Compson's account of Bon's reasons for replacing Judith's picture with the octoroon's: "And your old man wouldn't know about that too: why the black son of a bitch should have taken her picture out and put the octoroon's picture in, so he invented a reason for it" (358–59). The reason Shreve invents, on the other hand, shows Bon in a rather noble light: "It will be the only way I have to say to her, *I was no good; do not grieve for me*" (359). Shreve contests Mr. Compson's account even of such a simple matter as which of the two friends was injured in the war:

> Because your old man was wrong here, too! He said it was Bon who was wounded, but it wasn't. Because who told him? Who told Sutpen or your grandfather either, which of them it was who was hit? Sutpen didn't know because he wasn't there, and your grandfather wasn't there either because that was where he was hit too, where he lost his arm. So who told them? Not Henry, because his father never saw Henry but that one time and maybe they never had time to talk about wounds . . . and not Bon because Sutpen never saw Bon at all because he was dead—it was not Bon, it was Henry. (344)

Shreve thus discredits the reliability of the others, but what is his own source of authority? Surely he was not there either, so how does he know?[8]

Even about the central issue of the novel do the narrators dis-
agree. According to Rosa, Judith's marriage to Bon was forbid-
den "without rhyme or reason or shadow of excuse" (18);
according to Mr. Compson, the reason for the interdiction and
later for Henry's murder of Bon is Bon's impending bigamy (90);
but Quentin and Shreve see the obstacle first in the threat of incest
(293, 295–96) and later in miscegenation (355, 356).

With Quentin and Shreve, the novel explicitly replaces a view
of narration as representation by a conception of narration as
creation. To use Peter Brooks's formulation, "We have passed beyond any narrative reporting, to narrative invention . . . narrating, having failed to construct from the evidence a plot that would
make sense of the story, turns to inventing it" (1984, 303).
Whereas the narrators' absence from the events they narrate is an
obstacle to reliability when narration is seen as reporting or representation, it becomes an asset when narration is conceived of as
invention or imaginative creation: "And he, Quentin, could see
that too, though he had not been there—the ambulance with Miss
Coldfield between the driver and the second man . . . " (374–75);
or even stronger: "*If I had been there,*" Quentin thinks, "*I could
not have seen it this plain*" (190). Indeed, when the characters are
remote from the "facts," they become less reliable in the classical
sense and more creative. And, as the novel suggests, they come
closer to "the might have been that is more true than truth" (143).
The criterion for validity in this view is not a correspondence to
facts, but a narrative or artistic plausibility: "Does that suit you?"
Shreve asks Quentin at one point while embroidering the Judith-
Bon relationship (322). Narration becomes a game: "Let me play
a while now," we remember Shreve saying to his roommate
(280). That this view is endorsed by the extradiegetic narrator is
clear from such comments as: "four of them who sat in that drawing room [of Bon's mother] of baroque and fusty magnificence
which Shreve had invented and which was probably true enough"
(335); or "the slight dowdy woman with untidy gray-streaked

raven hair . . . which Shreve and Quentin had likewise invented and which was likewise probably true enough" (ibid.).

As if impelled by the uncanny logic of repetition, the readers reenact the experience of the narrators and, like them, replace reproduction by production. Faced with several different motives for the interdiction of the marriage between Judith and Bon, most critics opt for miscegenation. In order to explain how Quentin could know about this, however, they get involved in speculation. Lind, for example, suggests that Quentin's knowledge must have come from General Compson, who must have imparted to his grandson what he had withheld from Mr. Compson (1973, 281–82). Cleanth Brooks claims that Quentin may have heard the secret from Henry in their climactic meeting (1963, 316). Both critics rely on the following conversation between Quentin and Shreve:

> "He [Mr. Compson] didn't know it then. Grandfather didn't tell him all of it either, like Sutpen never told grandfather quite all of it."
> "Then who did tell him?"
> "I did. . . . The day after we—after that night when we——"
> (266)

The dialogue does indeed say that General Compson did not tell his son everything, but it does not say that he told Quentin, and since there is no conversation between the two in the entire novel, one can only invent it. Similarly, the climactic conversation between Henry and Quentin, as given in the text, consists of three questions and answers repeated twice and contains no information about either the interdiction or the miscegenation. To suggest a disclosure of the secret on Henry's part is to construct a scene the novel does not contain. Indeed, Shreve does imaginatively construct a scene when he "quotes" Sutpen saying to Henry: "He must not marry her, Henry . . . his mother was part negro" (354–

55).[9] And the critics follow suit, inferring, speculating, and inventing scenes, just like the fictional narrators whose limitations they analyze.[10]

Creation, rather than re-creation, does not only ripple out from the narrators to the readers-critics of the narrative but also ripples in from the narrators to the characters who are the objects of their narration. At the metadiegetic level, Bon is often described as a "shadow," a "phantom," "created" by the other characters—expressions that echo those referring to the act of storytelling on the part of the intradiegetic narrators. Rosa, for example, never saw Bon except in *"that photograph, that shadow, that picture in a young girl's bedroom"* (147), and yet she loved him, though—she says—*"not as women love. . . . Because even before I saw the photograph I could have recognized, nay, described the very face. But I never saw it. I do not even know of my own knowledge that Ellen ever saw it, that Judith ever loved it, that Henry slew it: so who will dispute me when I say, Why did I not invent, create it?"* (ibid.). Mr. Compson also comments on the quasi-fictional status of Bon in the Sutpen household: "Yes, shadowy: a myth, a phantom: something which they engendered and created whole themselves; some effluvium of Sutpen blood and character, as though as a man he did not exist at all" (104).[11] Even Bon's mother, according to Shreve, creates him in an image commensurate with her revenge plan: "until he got big enough to find out that it wasn't him at all she was washing and feeding the candy and the fun to but it was a man that hadn't even arrived yet, whom she had never seen yet" (306).

The mother's "creation" of her son as an instrument for her revenge is a manipulative exercise of power. No less manipulative is the lawyer's financially motivated creation. On the other hand, Rosa's invention of Bon is not so crudely manipulative, but she does need this phantom as an outlet for her repressed desire.[12] And Henry uses Bon both as a surrogate through whom he can make love to his own sister and as a homosexual love-object. In all these instances, the creation involves an attempt to control a situation or to dictate a scenario.

Critics have discerned an analogous power struggle at the level of intradiegetic narration. The Quentin-Shreve sections, for example, are not only a collaborative creation, but also a struggle for control over the narration: "'Wait, I tell you!' Quentin said, though still he did not move nor even raise his voice—that voice with its tense suffused restrained quality: 'I am telling'" (277); and Shreve retaliates a little later: "'No,' Shreve says, 'you wait. Let me play a while now'" (280).[13] Power also informs the reader's creative activity, to judge by such a description as Peter Brooks's: "What can this mean if not that the narratees/listeners/ readers have taken over complete responsibility for the narrative, and that the 'voice of the reader' has evicted all other voices from the text . . . in favour of a direct re-creation, and has set itself up, by a supreme act of usurpation, as the sole authority of narrative?" (304).

The power struggle may, I think, take on an additional dimension with the help of Judith's loom image. Like Mr. Compson's meditation, with which I started the chapter, Judith's speech is triggered by a letter—in fact, the same literal letter written by Bon, but again also "letter" as a metaphor for the erasure of voice in writing, and "letter" as an alphabetical character, a mark effaced on a tombstone. Judith starts by explaining her decision to give Bon's letter to Quentin's grandmother: "Because you make so little impression, you see" (127). This statement modulates into a vision of human beings as marionettes, all tied by the same strings, yet each trying to move independently. And the marionette image is then conflated with that of figures working at a loom: "like five or six people all trying to make a rug on the same loom only each one wants to weave his own pattern into the rug" (ibid.). This image—which, like Mr. Compson's metaphors, is also a *mise en abyme* of the narrative situation in *Absalom,*

Absalom!—obviously involves a power struggle. Each character, each narrator, wants to weave his own pattern into the same rug. But, in my opinion, the desire for power is here in the service of the desire to leave a mark (an image Judith uses a little later), to make room for an individual trace. And note that the "scratch," the "mark," does not depend on the content of the letter (the signified), not even on its being read, only on "passing from one hand to another" (ibid.), only—the Lacanian might say—on the itinerary of the signifier. It is thus not meaning or representation, but the very *act* of transmission, of telling, that may leave a trace, may save the individual from complete de-facement. This tentative affirmation of an individual mark coincides with Judith's only "speech" in the novel, making it a performance of its own content and linking the problem of representation with that of subjectivity.

Why is Judith granted a voice only once in the whole novel, and even then only at a metadiegetic level, quoted by Mr. Compson? Why aren't the other Sutpens used as narrators of their own story? Isn't it strange (or at least thought-provoking) that all the direct participants in the drama do not narrate,[14] whereas those who narrate do not participate directly?

Distance from the events often serves in this novel to stimulate the imaginative and creative faculties, and since narration—in one view in *Absalom, Absalom!*—is a production rather than a reproduction, it makes sense to assign the narrator's role to characters who did not take part in the experiences narrated. Taking this line of thinking a step further, one might suggest that absence, in addition to being a stimulus for the imagination, is also a precondition for language, since—from this perspective—language not only creates reality but replaces it. Such a view is no imposition of poststructuralist ideas on Faulkner's novel but emerges naturally from both *Absalom, Absalom!* and from other of Faulkner's works. In *As I Lay Dying*, Addie—speaking (appropriately) when she is already a corpse—sees language as a substitute for experience, and a poor substitute at that: "[Anse] had a word, too. Love, he called it. But I had been used to words for a long time. I knew that that word was like the others: just a shape to fill a lack" (136). It is a lack, an absence of experience, that gives rise to words: "sin and love and fear are just sounds that people who never sinned nor loved nor feared have for what they never had and cannot have until they forget the words" (133). Doesn't it follow, then, that those who did sin, love, and fear would have no need to talk about it, whereas those who did not, would?

Opposed to Addie's view of language as a mere frame for absences is her praise of "voiceless words," i.e., direct, nonverbal contact. Similarly, in *Absalom, Absalom!* when Clytie touches Rosa, the physical contact is so overwhelming that it cuts through all social and linguistic conventions: "Because there is something in the touch of flesh with flesh which abrogates, cuts sharp and straight across the devious channels of decorous ordering, which enemies as well as lovers know because it makes them both— touch and touch of that which is the citadel of the central I-Am's private own: not spirit, soul" (139). Rosa here relates touch to the notion of an essential self, "the central I Am's private own." Without a belief in essences or in selves, Bon also acknowledges the overwhelming power of nonverbal communication. He is therefore dismayed that the meeting with his father produces "no shock, no hot communicated flesh that speech would have been too slow even to impede" (320; see also 348). And between Judith and Sutpen there is an intimate understanding that dispenses with words: "They did not need to talk. They were too much alike. They were as two people become now and then, who seem to know one another so well or are so much alike that the power, the need, to communicate by speech atrophies from disuse and, comprehending without need of the medium of ear or intellect, they no longer understand one another's actual words" (122).[15]

Language becomes superfluous in the presence of physical reality, language replaces reality, language creates reality—these related varieties of a nonrepresentational view of language can all explain the split between doing and telling that informs the choice of narrators in *Absalom, Absalom!* Explanations of a different order emerge from a psychological, rather than a philosophical, orientation. Judith's "loom speech" is an example of this orientation. If narration is one way of making a mark, then the denial of the narrator's role to the Sutpens may be an indication of their marionette-like status, of the hopelessness of attempting to disentangle the strings attached to one individual from those fastened to the others.

If "trying to tell" implies some faith in the possibility of communication, the Sutpens' exclusion from the narrator's position may reflect their distrust of interpersonal discourse. McPherson relates such distrust to Thomas Sutpen's childhood trauma, the trauma of not being allowed to deliver a message to the plantation owner. This scene is repeatedly referred to as Sutpen's loss of innocence and as the origin of his design. What Sutpen learned in this episode, McPherson argues, is "that a teller is inevitably limited by the other's desire or willingness to listen" (1987, 439), and since the other was not willing to listen, Sutpen's belief in communication was shattered. "Disappointed innocence led to an extreme distrust of exchange, a cynicism that must inevitably deform the narrative tradition" (ibid., 440). Sutpen then turns to the world of action, attempting to make a mark through his deeds, his design. As we know, this design causes the exclusion— the silencing—of Bon, but also, according to McPherson, the verbal incapacitation of his whole family: "Thus, Thomas Sutpen, concerned above all with building and leaving a legacy, guaranteed the verbal sterility of his children" (ibid.). His children can speak only without speaking: Clytie's face, Henry's absence, Jim Bond's howling.[16]

In the foregoing hypotheses non-narration is seen as crippling, but a different perspective reveals that silence, like narration, can become a tool in a power struggle. Sutpen is again the most prominent example. In fact, the success of his design depends on people's being in the dark about his origins, his past, his actions: "So they would catch him, run him to earth in the lounge between the supper table and his locked door to give him the opportunity to tell them who he was and where he came from and what he was up to, whereupon he would move gradually and steadily until his back came in contact with something—a post or a wall—and then stand there and tell them nothing whatever as pleasantly and courteously as a hotel clerk" (34).

The exception to Sutpen's reticence is his one narration—significantly reported at a meta-metadiegetic level—to General Compson. But just as his silence was motivated by a desire to gain the upper hand, so his narration serves the need to control, to restore his power by discovering the mistake that undermined his design.

Sutpen's habitual silence provokes the narrative faculties of the other characters, giving rise to many stories about him. The Sutpen myth, and to a large extent even Sutpen's subjectivity, is a collection of stories others tell about him. Even when telling his own story to General Compson, Sutpen talks as if he were another, almost as if he were inventing a narrative: "Since he was not talking about himself. He was telling a story. He was not bragging about something he had done; he was just telling a story about something a man named Thomas Sutpen had experienced, which would still have been the same story if the man had no name at all, if it had been told about any man or no man over whiskey at night" (247).

The dissociation between narrating subject and narrated object takes two complementary forms in *Absalom, Absalom!* On the one hand, the subjectivity of the non-narrating characters becomes a construction by others. You are what others say about you. On the other hand, the narrators' access to their own subjectivity is achieved through their narration about others. You are what you say about others. This is so because talking about others in this novel is normally not a constative reproduction but a performative production, a transference-like repetition that is itself a performative *act* in the present. Whatever degree of subjectivity Quentin and Shreve accede to, they do by "living," enacting, the objects of their narration, whom they create in their own image and according to their own needs.[17]

A disruption of the expected correlation between utterances and speakers causes further problematization of the relation between narration and subjectivity. Although I made a preliminary identification of the various narrators in *Absalom, Absalom!* earlier, the novel abounds in features of discourse that make it often difficult, if not impossible, to attribute utterances to speakers. Analysis of one particularly perplexing segment (181–216) may shed light on other problematic instances.[18] The segment occurs at the beginning of the Quentin-Shreve narration, just after Shreve's ironic summary of the Sutpen saga and Quentin's laconic reply, "Yes" (181). The assent is followed by an internal comment, "He sounds just like father," a comment that bridges the transition into Quentin's consciousness, further marked by "thought" and "thinking" as well as by the change to italics (ibid.). We seem to remain inside Quentin's consciousness for three and a half pages, though we are sometimes bewildered by the tone, which is more like Shreve's than Quentin's, and by expressions that are specifically Shreve's (e.g., "the Creditor"). At the end of this long stretch, Quentin suddenly speaks aloud, confirming the foregoing account: "'Yes,' Quentin said" (185). Since it is unlikely—though not impossible—that Quentin would now audibly confirm his own silent thinking, the reader tentatively attributes the italicized pages to Shreve, an attribution that coheres with the tone and idiom of the problematic sections but clashes with the earlier markers of transition into Quentin's thoughts.

Confused by conflicting clues, the reader may try to reconcile them by hypothesizing that the italicized segment renders

Quentin's memories of Shreve's narration, preserving the salient
characteristics of Shreve's style.[19] Quentin's assent to his own
memories still feels strange, but it does mark the sequel (185–87)
as Shreve's, though this marking becomes indeterminate when on
page 187 a segment not in italics opens with "How was it?"
Shreve said. "You told me; how was it." Shreve's parenthetical
voice then gives way to what seems like the extradiegetic narrator
telling about Quentin's visit to the graveyard with his father
(188). But where has Shreve gone? And how does one account for
comments like, "It seemed to Quentin that he could actually see
them: the ragged and starving troops without shoes" (189). One
way of accounting for such consciousness markers is to see the
whole segment from page 188 to page 216 as the narrator's verbalization of Quentin's thoughts. (In this view, the voice is the
narrator's; Quentin is the focalizer.) But one is brought up short
by sentences bearing Mr. Compson's stylistic stamp as well as by
such statements as "though your grandfather of course did not
know this" (191), "And your grandfather never knew if it was
Clytie who watched" (195), "Your grandfather didn't know"
(200, 201, 202). Now the speaking voice seems to be Mr.
Compson's. Or are these memories Quentin has of his father's
narration when he is looking at his father's letter? This possibility
seems to be supported by the return to Shreve—and the present—
on page 207, through Quentin's italicized thoughts: *"Yes. I have
heard too much; I have had to listen to too much, too long* thinking *"Yes, Shreve sounds almost exactly like father: that letter."*
The passage continues with Quentin's thoughts, but page 208
seems to return to Mr. Compson's voice (or Quentin's memory of
it), and page 210 comes back to Quentin's consciousness with
"Yes," he thought, *"too much too long."* Page 211 repeats the
same idea, adding *"because he sounds just like father,"* which
seems to lead either into Shreve's speech (without changing the
italics, however) or into Quentin's memories of Shreve's narration. Expressions like "your father" (213) and "Shreve said" sug-

gest that Shreve is actually speaking, as does Quentin's rejoinder "Yes," on page 215. Shreve then continues telling Quentin what Quentin had previously told him, though now without italics, up to the end of chapter 6.

The effect of complexity is increased when we realize that even utterances by an unambiguously specified speaker are colored by what Bakhtin calls "the language of the other." Examine, for example, the early internal dialogue between "two separate Quentins now talking to one another in the long silence of not-people, in notlanguage, like this":

> *It seems that this demon—his name was Sutpen—(Colonel Sutpen)—Colonel Sutpen. Who came out of nowhere and without warning upon the land with a band of strange niggers and built a plantation (Tore violently a plantation, Miss Rosa Coldfield says)—tore violently. And married her sister Ellen and begot a son and a daughter which (Without gentleness begot, Miss Rosa Coldfield says)—without gentleness. Which should have been the jewels of his pride and the shield and comfort of his old age, only—(Only they destroyed him or something or he destroyed them or something. And died)— and died. Without regret, Miss Rosa Coldfield says—(Save by her) Yes, save by her. (And by Quentin Compson). Yes. And by Quentin Compson. (9)*

It is easy to see how Quentin's thoughts are infiltrated by Rosa's language. This is one of many instances of the superimposition of voices in *Absalom, Absalom!*

A further complication of the traditionally assumed tie between narration and an originating self results from the overall uniformity of the style, in spite of the specific tone, expressions, and linguistic idiosyncrasies that characterize each narrator. Peter Brooks describes this phenomenon: "Narration here as elsewhere in Faulkner seems to call upon both the individual's voice and that transindividual voice that speaks through all of

Faulkner's characters" (1984, 294). Such uniformity is problematic for the view of narration as representation, since "the Mimetic Language Game" (to use Moshe Ron's felicitous expression [1981, 17–39]) assumes that each narrator (and each character) has a characteristic way of speaking, and that one can therefore attribute all utterances to particular speakers.[20]

Disturbed by the disruption of traditional assumptions, some critics attempt a redistribution of utterances to preserve plausibility. Toker, for example, argues that "what the reader hears is not the voices of these speakers but the voice of the omniscient narrator carrying their narrative acts in their stead" (1993, 160).[21] Waggoner (1966) and Irwin (1975), on the other hand, suggest that the first five chapters are Quentin's memories when he is alone in his Harvard room, roused by his father's announcement of Rosa's death to recall conversations with him as well as with the old maid. In chapter 6 Shreve enters and together they go over the story once more (Waggoner 1966, 177).[22]

While Toker, Waggoner, and Irwin use narrative strategies to rehabilitate a representational reading of *Absalom, Absalom!* others reject representation—and claim that Faulkner does the same. Krause (1984, 230), for example, sees *Absalom, Absalom!* as advocating the "ceaseless play of signification" (238) rather than "the reductions" of referentiality, representation, and closure. The disconnection between language and individual voice is, according to him, an aspect of the same predilection: "Consequently, the reader faces the radical situation described by Barthes in *S/Z:* 'The more indeterminate the origin of the statement, the more plural the text. In modern texts, the voices are so treated that any reference is impossible: the discourse, or better, the language, speaks: nothing more'" (Krause 1984, 235).

Representation, however, returns if one sees the confusion of voices not only as a sign of the novel's textuality but as a rendering of the merging or the interchangeability of characters. The similarity between Shreve's and Quentin's narration, for example, is analogous to the interchangeability of their roles and selves: "They stared—glared—at one another. It was Shreve speaking, though save for the slight difference which the intervening degrees of latitude had inculcated in them (differences not in tone or pitch but of turn of phrases and usage of words), it might have been either of them and was in a sense both: both thinking as one, the voice which happened to be speaking the thought only the thinking become audible, vocal" (303). From this perspective, identification of the voice is immaterial, because it is only the vocal realization of thoughts shared by the two narrators. And the thoughts are common to both for two reasons. First, Quentin and Shreve have come to represent a universal quality beyond their personal existence: "the two who breathed not individuals now yet something both more and less than twins, the heart and blood of youth" (294). Second, listening is no less creative than telling; the narratee thus becomes another narrator: "That was why it did not matter to either of them which one did the talking, since it was not the talking alone which did it, performed and accomplished the overpassing, but some happy marriage of speaking and hearing" (316).

As narrators, Quentin and Shreve are not only interchangeable with each other but also with Henry and Bon, the objects of their narration. This is emphasized by a series of analogies and metalepses between narrative levels. Just as Quentin and Shreve interrupt each other with a recurrent "wait, wait," so they attribute the same expression to the people they discuss: "And then it was Bon that said, 'Wait' . . . and Henry said 'Wait. Wait. I must have time to get used to it'" (340).[23] The boundaries between levels blur when Shreve's description of Henry as "panting and looking, glaring at the sky" is followed by the extradiegetic narrator's comment that, in telling this, Shreve is "(glaring at Quentin, panting himself, as if he had had to supply his shade not only with a cue but also with breath to obey it in)" (344). It is as if Shreve and Henry are at the same narrative level, and Shreve can supply Henry with breath through his own panting.

The fusion between narrators and objects of narration is not only implicitly suggested by analogies and metalepses. It is also explicitly formulated on many occasions: "in the cold room where there was now not two of them but four" (294); "not two of them there and then either but four of them riding the two horses through the iron darkness" (295); "four of them and then just two—Charles-Shreve and Quentin-Henry" (334).[24]

The network of identifications is further expanded by the inclusion of Mr. Compson. Reacting to Shreve's narration, Quentin thinks: *"He sounds just like father. . . . Just exactly like father if father had known as much about it the night before I went out there as he did the night after I came back"* (181). And Shreve detects the same affinity between Quentin and his father: "'Don't say it's just me that sounds like your old man' Shreve said" (261). The fusion of voices belonging to different generations may be interpreted as a sign of the helplessness of the individual in the grip of temporal repetition. This, Irwin argues, "is the form that the fate or doom of a family takes in Faulkner" (1975, 61). Such, indeed, is Quentin's understanding of the resemblance: *"Yes. Maybe we are both Father. Maybe nothing ever happens once and is finished. . . . Yes, we are both Father. Or maybe Father and I are both Shreve, maybe it took Father and me both to make Shreve or Shreve and me both to make Father or maybe Thomas Sutpen to make all of us"* (261–62). This inescapability makes even the first narration a repetition of things already known instinctively: *"But you were not listening, because you knew it all already, had learned, absorbed it already without the medium of speech somehow from having been born and living beside it, with it, as children will and do: so that what your father was saying did not tell you anything so much as it struck, word by word, the resonant strings of remembering"* (213).

From this angle, what Brooks described as "that transindividual voice that speaks through all of Faulkner's characters," and what Toker labeled the voice of the omniscient narrator, is the voice of the South, of all the ghosts in the air of the region and in the blood of its inhabitants. Such an engulfment of the personal voice by the collective undermines the very notion of self as a unique being: "His [Quentin's] childhood was full of them; his very body was an empty hall echoing with sonorous defeated names; he was not a being, an entity, he was a commonwealth. He was a barracks filled with stubborn back-looking ghosts still recovering, even forty-three years afterwards, from the fever which had cured the disease" (12). It is against this loss of voice that the characters engage in narration, perhaps the only way of refusing "at last to be a ghost" (362).[25] Although full-fledged, autonomous selves (in the traditional sense) have become impossible in this novel, the character-narrators do at least "make a mark" (127), a mark that invites other characters (as well as generations of critics) to try to decipher, or invent, "what the scratches were trying to tell" (ibid.), and in the process gain some access to subjectivity.

This chapter has analyzed conflicting views of representation and subjectivity in *Absalom, Absalom!* by concentrating on the intricacies of narration. As should be clear by now, narration is central not only in this novel but also in my attempt to offer a new approach to representation and subjectivity. However, at the end of the chapter, it may be interesting to shift the focus somewhat and relate these concerns to the specific story *Absalom, Absalom!* tells. I realize, of course, that this is a tricky undertaking, given the proliferation of narrators and the problems of reliability/creation, which make it difficult to abstract any story with any degree of certainty. Nevertheless, in spite of its problematic status and many inherent contradictions, the Sutpen saga obsesses all the narrators and therefore seems to qualify as the novel's hypothetical story. It is both as the novel's "story" and as the story of history that the saga deserves our attention here.

One can draw two analogies between Sutpen's adventures and the adventures of narrating (and reading) them.[26] The first relates inaccessibilities and exclusions in Sutpen's life to gaps as obstacles to the representational endeavor. The second compares Sutpen's attempt to fashion a self and a world with the view of narration as creation.

Sutpen's life abounds in exclusions, absences, and obscurities. Just such an experience, a barred door and no permission to deliver a message to the plantation owner, puts an end to his proverbial innocence. To ensure that he never again becomes a victim of exclusion, Sutpen develops a design that itself involves a brutal exclusion of any possible obstacle, notably his partly black wife and their son, Charles Bon. Putting the past behind him, Sutpen starts anew in a place where he is very careful to keep his origins in total darkness. Here he goes about founding a dynasty, casting aside nonwinners like Milly Jones, who bears him a daughter when his plan required a son.

The exclusions, secrets, and absences characterizing Sutpen's life are uncannily similar to the gaps that thwart the narrators' reconstructive efforts. And like the narrators, who initially tried to figure out letters and events, readers—especially those with Compson-like expectations—find themselves barred from knowledge. The reading process, like narration, becomes a performative repetition of the thing it is trying to decipher. Readers take the position of Sutpen's victims, although only to an extent, for, as we remember, Sutpen himself was initially a victim of obstruction. By making the readers relive, "perform," both Sutpen's trauma and the traumas he inflicts on others, the novel promotes complexity of moral and psychological response.

The second analogy—arguably the obverse of the first—hinges on the role of creation in Sutpen's life, as well as in the Quentin-Shreve collaboration. Sutpen's design, not unlike that of the Quentin-Shreve narration, is an attempt to turn an imaginative conception into a reality, to create the world in the shape of his desires. It is also an attempt to create himself, a process of self-fashioning. But Sutpen's creation crumbles, and it crumbles precisely because of the return of the repressed, the coming back of the excluded Bon. The ensuing Bon-Henry-Judith triangle and its tragic consequences end Sutpen's hopes for a dynasty and destroy his creation from within. The Quentin-Shreve creation, on the other hand, thrives and survives as "the might have been that is more true than truth." Perhaps the dialogic character of the Quentin-Shreve creation, as opposed to Sutpen's dependence on an exclusion of others in fashioning himself, explains their success and his failure.[27] Access to subjectivity, this would suggest, necessitates an inclusion of the other.

The analogies discussed so far concern the personal aspect of Sutpen's life. But the personal story is intertwined with the history of the Civil War and the tragedy of the South. In this respect, too, *Absalom, Absalom!* is under the sign of conflict. The novel presents history as the origin of all the other predicaments it dramatizes. By implication, an understanding of history could provide the ultimate explanation, the ultimate something that is otherwise always missing. But the reconstruction of history is no less fraught with difficulties than the reproduction of the story. It too is haunted by absences, has to content itself with hypotheses instead of facts, and is inhabited by creation and fictionality. The chain of narrators and the multiplicity of narrative levels in *Absalom, Absalom!* both interrogate traditional views of history and emphasize its narrativity, even fictionality, in a way that anticipates current approaches.

Absalom, Absalom! thus effects a rapprochement between history and story and an analogy between their destabilization and the vicissitudes of narration. Whereas the relation between self and other, central to the analogy between Sutpen's self-creation and the Quentin-Shreve narration, links *Absalom, Absalom!* with *The Real Life of Sebastian Knight,* the complex concern with history has an affinity with a later text in this study, namely *Beloved.* Like *Absalom, Absalom!, Beloved* multiplies narrative levels, but—in spite of the integration of destabilization—it does so in

order to re-engage with representation and subjectivity and to re-
trieve history via fiction. The similarities and differences between
these two texts will become apparent in a later chapter. In the
meantime, I wish to suggest once again that, in the tension it
stages between the epistemological yearning for reliability and
verifiability and the ontological game of world-making,
Absalom, Absalom! is a transitional text between modernism and
postmodernism. *Beloved,* on the other hand, is a partial reaction
against postmodernism from within. But this is a further glance
beyond doubt, and a subject for a separate discussion.

3

Vladimir Nabokov, *The Real Life of Sebastian Knight*
"The painting of different ways of painting"

As in *Absalom, Absalom!*, the exploration of the possibilities and limitations of representation in *The Real Life of Sebastian Knight* takes the form of an attempt to reconstruct the past and its inevitable discontents. In both novels, the past emerges from, or is created by, a kaleidoscope of stories told by different narrators and gleaned from various characters. This situation, with its unsettling implications for the status of narration, is foregrounded by the use of *mise en abyme*. Judith's loom image from *Absalom, Absalom!* is comparable in this respect to V's characterization of Sebastian's *The Prismatic Bezel*. Judith visualizes "five or six people all trying to make a rug on the same loom only each one wants to weave his own pattern into the rug" (127). And the image V borrows from painting similarly emphasizes the collage principle that, according to him, informs Sebastian's novel: "It is as if a painter said: Look, here I'm going to show you not the painting of a landscape, but the painting of different ways of painting a certain landscape, and I trust their harmonious fusion will disclose the landscape as I intend you to see it" (79).[1]

In both cases, the idea of a stable reality is replaced by a multiplicity of subjective perceptions. Whether these perceptions ultimately represent reality remains an open question in both *Absalom, Absalom!* and *The Real Life of Sebastian Knight,* corresponding (at least in part) to whether the subjective versions are grasped as unreliable or are invested with the truth of imaginative creation.

The past reconstructed or constructed in these novels is, to a large extent, the life history of an individual or group of individuals, and the attempt to represent reality is related (more in *The Real Life of Sebastian Knight* than in *Absalom, Absalom!*) to the project of representing a "real life" of a certain individual. But the relation between narration and subjectivity is no less problematic than that between narration and representation. To begin with, does narration render a preexisting, autonomous self, or does it constitute a subject in the very act of telling? Moreover, does narration convey or constitute the subject it tells about (Sutpen, Henry, Bon, Sebastian Knight) or the subjectivity of the teller (Quentin, Shreve, V), or both? These less than simple questions are further complicated by the performative character of narration in both novels. In talking about Henry and Bon, Quentin and Shreve actually live what they narrate/create, repeating the absent past in the present of their own lives. Similarly, in searching for the real life of his half brother, V's narration causes him to reenact that life. Quentin and Shreve "become" Henry and Bon just as V "becomes" Sebastian Knight.

Since *The Real Life of Sebastian Knight* pursues and interrogates the problematic quest of reality mainly through the search for the "real life" of its title character, I shall start with the problem of subjectivity, and only later broaden the exploration to the issue of representation. Characters at different narrative levels of

The Real Life of Sebastian Knight explicitly state opposed views of subjectivity. *Lost Property,* Sebastian's autobiographical novel, presents a traditional image of the self as a unique, inalienable inner essence: "I seem to pass with intangible steps across ghostly lawns and through dancing halls full of the whine of Hawaiian music and down dear drab little streets with pretty names, until I come to a certain warm hollow where something very like the selfest of my own self sits huddled up in the darkness" (58).

Nothing sounds more alien to "the selfest of [one's] own self" than V's discovery of the possibility of freedom from the straitjacket of personality: "Whatever his [Sebastian's] secret was, I have learnt one secret too, and namely: that the soul is but a manner of being—not a constant state—that any soul may be yours, if you find and follow its undulations. The hereafter may be the full ability of consciously living in any chosen soul, in any number of souls, all of them unconscious of their interchangeable burden" (172). However, these seemingly contradictory views have more in common than meets the eye. The self discovered in *Lost Property* is actually a double who sits huddled up in the darkness while the "I" walks the streets. This self is thus alienated or displaced through the other; from this perspective it is another. Conversely, the freedom V envisions is a series of transitory identifications by which one gains access to subjectivity through the other.

The problem of subjectivity, as well as its relation to otherness, is enacted through the troubled identities of the narrator and the object of his narration. Both V and Sebastian may be conceived of as narrators; both may also be considered objects of narration. The novel gives rise to these two possibilities, together with several subcategories, and renders choice impossible. The coexistence of opposed hypotheses dramatizes a complex attitude to subjectivity via narration.

Let me begin with the sharper incompatibility. Until almost the end of the novel, V seems the ostensible narrator. However, the climactic identification at the end—"Thus I am Sebastian

Knight" (172)—in retrospective conjunction with the casually imparted information that Sebastian's intention to write a fictional biography had never materialized ("That was a book Sebastian never wrote" [34]) suggest that the "unwritten" text may be the novel we read. In other words, *The Real Life of Sebastian Knight* may be Sebastian's autobiography, and V merely a persona. Such a twist is perfectly congruent with Sebastian's playful cast of mind, and the use of V as a mask for the "real" author tallies with Sheldon's statement that Sebastian's novels are "but bright masks" (87). Various critics have discussed the possibility of a switch from V as narrator of Sebastian's biography to Sebastian as author of an autobiography using V as narrator. Dabney Stuart says: "For the narrator, the person whose perspective we are left with at the end of the novel is, as we discover, Sebastian himself" (1968, 313). And Andrew Field asks: "Is it possible that *The Real Life of Sebastian Knight* is not a biography at all, but a fictional autobiography, another of Knight's novels?" (quoted in Bruffee 1973, 181).

The clash between V and Sebastian as potential candidates for the role of narrator is also a clash between seeing the novel as biography or as autobiography. The biography/autobiography dichotomy, however, is not limited to the ambiguity of the narrator. Even if we take V as an uncontested narrator (a decision the novel does not authorize), the object of his narration remains an open question. The title arouses expectations of a biography, either fictional or real. In accordance with traditional generic conventions, we expect the narrator to describe a third person's development. The first paragraph, however, already frustrates these expectations by containing seven first-person and only two third-person pronouns, an imbalance that gets aggravated as the text progresses. As Charles Nicol puts it, "The more V talks about his half brother the less we seem to know about him" (1967, 88). At the same time, the more V talks about his half brother, the more we seem to know about V. Is the novel, then, about Sebastian's life or about V's quest for Sebastian's life? Is it Sebastian's biography or V's autobiography?

The polarity in this case is less clear-cut than the ambiguity of the narrator's identity. Here the two possibilities are not mutually exclusive, and the contrast between them may be complicated by a discrepancy between intention and execution. V may have intended to write a biography but ended up unwittingly composing an autobiography—in which case the execution might be judged by the reader as a failure in relation to the intention and/or as the triumph of unconscious motivations. V says: "As the reader may have noticed, I have tried to put into this book as little of my own self as possible" (117). The reader, however, has noticed no such thing and is therefore likely to adopt an ironic attitude toward V's statements. Beyond the irony, though, s/he may try to understand the unconscious reasons underlying the discrepancy between declared intention and execution. Could it be V's narcissism, his need to make room for himself in Sebastian's biography, or his desire to become a part of Sebastian's *life*? Support for the second hypothesis comes from V's reaction to Goodman's biography of Sebastian: "Oddly enough, this second marriage [of Sebastian's father] is not mentioned at all in Mr. Goodman's *Tragedy of Sebastian Knight* . . . so that to readers of Goodman's book I am bound to appear non-existent" (6). Consequently, when V assures us that "if I continue to harp on the subject [of Goodman], I do so for Sebastian Knight's sake" (52), we may conjecture that it is precisely for his own sake that he attacks Goodman; in order to rectify his nonexistence in Goodman's biography, he writes an account easily transformable into autobiography. In a way that recalls the various narrators of *Absalom, Absalom!*, V's struggle for control over the narration may also be a struggle for self-assertion. Moreover, V's unconscious motivation may extend beyond the biography to the life itself. Various details in the novel suggest that during Sebastian's lifetime, contact between the two half brothers was minimal (cf. 14, 15, 26–27, 164), so it is plausible that V would unconsciously try to insert himself into Sebastian's life in retrospect by writing (or rewriting) the story. More sinister is the possibility that V is unconsciously taking revenge on Sebastian for his "constant aloofness" (15) by manipulating his biography, now that Sebastian is dead and V controls the narrative.

So far I have elaborated on the hypothesis that V is the narrator, Sebastian the intended object of narration, but V himself the actual, unwitting, object of narration. But the autobiography may also have been intended by V, as some critics suggest, in which case there is no discrepancy between intention and execution. "Certainly," says K. A. Bruffee, "this novel is not the fictional biography it claims to be. The title is a ruse. Sebastian Knight is not the center of attention at all, although he is, or *was,* the narrator's center of attention . . . the novel is a fictional autobiography. Its subject is V, the narrator" (1973, 181). Various conscious reasons may have led V to write his own story through Sebastian's, for example, the knowledge (expressed on several occasions) that Sebastian is the more famous of the two and the book may therefore gain in interest by purporting to be about him, or even an experimental play—on the part of a self-conscious narrator—with the borders between biography and autobiography.

Having discussed the alternative narrators and their intended or unintended objects of narration, an explicit expansion on the contribution of these phenomena to the problematics of subjectivity and narration is now in order. On the face of it, the biography hypothesis sees narration as the (re)construction of the subjectivity of an other, whereas the autobiography hypothesis views it as a (re)construction of one's own subjectivity. The coexistence of both hypotheses,[2] however, seems to be a performative articulation of both the alienation of the subject through the other and the constitution of the other through the narrating subject.

Indeed, "the merging of twin images" is explicitly formulated by the narrator in the final sentence of the novel: "I am Sebastian, or Sebastian is I, or perhaps we both are someone whom neither of us knows" (172). To relate this insight back to the foregoing hypotheses, if V purports to write Sebastian's biography and ends up (unwittingly?) writing his own, narrating the other's life makes him discover his own subjectivity. But the quest and the telling make him discover that he is another—Sebastian. If the novel is Sebastian's autobiography, using V as a persona, then the narration explores subjectivity through the other, but also otherness through subjectivity, since V as Sebastian's narrating persona is in quest of the real life of Sebastian Knight. . . . In both cases, there emerges an identification of the subject with the other, coupled with an alienation or displacement of the subject through the other. This is a structure reminiscent of Lacan's description of the mirror stage, in which the reflection is recognized as both identical to and different from the face looking at it, and mirror images abound in this novel.

The novel's title, with which I started the discussion of the relations between narration and subjectivity, also opens up the question of representation. For, in addition to arousing expectations of a biography, the novel's title implies the possibility of reaching reality and telling about it. Readers familiar with Nabokov's work may detect an ironic overtone in this title, which has the ring of a cliché characteristic of certain popular genres. V's later thoughts give an indirect ironic twist to the title: "Oh, how I sometimes yearn for the easy swing of a well-oiled novel! . . . A handy character, a welcome passer-by who had also known my hero, but from a different angle. 'And now,' he would say, 'I am going to tell you the real story of Sebastian Knight's college years'" (44). Doesn't this suggest that *The Real Life* . . . is possible only in well-oiled, facile novels and that reality is much more evanescent than such titles would lead one to believe?

This double movement, whereby a glimpse of reality is—as

Barthes would say—*posé et deçu,* goes beyond the title to characterize the entire novel. The possibility of an "extraordinary revelation" about reality (164), about "the real life," although emerging at various narrative levels, is also suspect or unattainable. A sense that "now the puzzle was solved" (150) permeates the final scene of Sebastian's *The Doubtful Asphodel,* leading both characters and readers to expect "some absolute truth," "the absolute solution" (149, 150) from the lips of the dying man. But a moment's hesitation on the part of the author proves fatal: "The man is dead and we do not know" (151). Similarly, V dreams that Sebastian "was calling me and saying something very important—and promising to tell me something more important still, if only I came to the corner where he sat or lay, trapped by the heavy sacks that had fallen across his legs" (159). But the "striking disclosure" takes the form of a "garbled sentence" (160), which V cannot understand. Under the shock of this dream, V travels to the St. Damier hospital, which he reaches only after Sebastian's death. Like Sebastian's novel, like V's dream, Sebastian's life ends without disclosing the ultimate secret. This gap, this absence, motivates V's quest for the real life of his half brother and his need to narrate it.

The impulse to pin down reality, to represent the absence, is questioned in the novel in a variety of ways. First, is it desirable to represent reality? Sebastian's "real life," like his prose, "was a dazzling succession of gaps; and you cannot ape a gap because you are bound to fill it in somehow or other—and blot it out in the process" (30). Second, is it possible to represent reality? Like the narrators in *Absalom, Absalom!* V has very limited contact with the "real life" he is trying to narrate, so he necessarily resorts to assembling information from the stories other characters tell him (Sebastian's governess, Sheldon, Miss Pratt, Nina Rechnoy-Lecerf, etc.). As in *Absalom, Absalom!,* here too the informants suffer from limited knowledge, difficulties in remembering the

past, distorting emotional involvement, and even downright in-
sincerity. This creates a problem of reliability, which V formu-
lates on behalf of a mysterious Voice in the Mist, the voice of
conscience asking, "Who is speaking of Sebastian Knight?": "It
was but the echo of some possible truth, a timely reminder: don't
be too certain of learning the past from the lips of the present. Be-
ware of the most honest broker. Remember that what you are
told is really threefold: shaped by the teller, reshaped by the listener, concealed from both by the dead man of the tale" (44).
Third, if the "real life" is a piecing together of various stories, is it
anything more than a narrative, a fiction? And if the various unintended fictions fail to represent reality, what is the status of
Sebastian's self-declared fictions, his novels? The conflict between narration as representation and narration as creation, so
noticeable in *Absalom, Absalom!,* is enriched in *The Real Life of
Sebastian Knight* by the tension between reality and fictionality.
This tension emerges from analogies between Sebastian's novels
and Sebastian's life, as well as from those between Sebastian's
novels and V's quest. The first set of analogies seems to reinforce
the view of narration as representation (Sebastian's novels are
molded on his own life), while the second seems to suggest that
narration creates—rather than re-creates—reality (Sebastian's
novels determine the form and development of V's quest).

Let me begin with the first set. A certain passage in *Success* is
said to be "strangely connected with Sebastian's inner life at the
time of the completing of the last chapter" (82), but no details are
given about the nature of the connection. In the same novel,
though, William, the protagonist, suffers from his heart and con-
sults a doctor named Coates (ibid.). Sebastian also has a heart disease; his doctor is called Oates (88). The unrealized meetings in
Success (81) and the near confrontation between Sebastian and
Clare by the Charing Cross bookstall (154) are analogous as well.
In Sebastian's short story *The Back of the Moon,* the "meek little

man" is reminiscent of another "meek little man" who provoked a tremendous scene of rage and fury by unwittingly interrupting Sebastian in his work (85).

Lost Property, supposedly an autobiographical novel, is generally similar to Sebastian's life. Particularly analogous is the situation in which a man breaks up a happy love affair for the sake of a fatal and miserable one, "the damned formula of 'another woman'" (93). V considers that the letter written by a character in *Lost Property* on this occasion resembles what Sebastian felt about Clare or perhaps even wrote to her, although the twin character is a faintly absurd one.

Doubtful Asphodel, composed when Sebastian is mortally ill, reenacts the anxiety of a man who fears he will die before revealing the great truth he has glimpsed. Small details in this novel, for example Clare's silver shoes (86, 147) and the feeling of regret for not giving a penny to an old beggar (90, 148), also parallel Sebastian's life.

Sebastian's novels thus seem to render his life in a representational mode. But the Voice in the Mist explicitly warns against such a simplistic view: "Who is speaking of Sebastian Knight? . . . Who indeed? His best friend and his half brother. A gentle scholar, remote from life, and an embarrassed traveller visiting a distant land. And where is the third party? Rotting peacefully in the cemetery of St. Damier. Laughingly alive in five volumes" (44). Sebastian may be more alive in his novels than in his life, and the hierarchy implied by the traditional representational view is questioned.

The analogies between Sebastian's novels and V's quest place the traditional representational view much more heavily under fire, for beyond a suggestion of the supremacy of fiction over the writer's own life, they signal the capacity of fiction to mold the reality of another. Sebastian's first novel, *The Prismatic Bezel,* is, among other things, "a rollicking parody of the setting of a detective tale" (76) and hence full of "false scents" and delays: "Owing to a combination of mishaps (his car runs over an old woman and then he takes the wrong train) the detective is very long in arriving" (77). V's quest is similarly a process of detection (minus the parody) with its own false scents, like Mr. Goodman, and its own delays, like Mme Lecerf and the various obstacles put in V's path to the dying Sebastian: a slow car, a wrong turning, and all the rest of the conventional retardatory apparatus. In any self-respecting detective novel, the murderer turns out to be the one least suspected by the police and the reader. *The Prismatic Bezel* takes this device to a ridiculous extreme. The corpse is that of an art dealer called G. Abeson. In the crowd there is a passerby, the harmless old Nosebag, who has a passion for collecting snuffboxes. When the detective finally arrives and starts cross-questioning everybody, a policeman suddenly informs him that the corpse is gone. Old Nosebag now steps forward, taking off his beard, wig, and spectacles, to reveal the face of G. Abeson. The most harmless looking among the crowd turns out to be not the murderer, as in the conventional detective story, but the murdered. The newly resurrected corpse then goes on to explain: "You see . . . one dislikes being murdered" (79). Abeson's death is transcended by his identification with the living Nosebag. A similar situation, in a serious vein, occurs at the beginning of V's quest.[3] Sebastian is no more; yet disliking being dead, he is continued by a death-transcending duplicate in the person of his half brother, V: "I am Sebastian Knight."[4] In both cases the identification is connected with the names of the two parties. "Nosebag" is the exact reversal of "G. Abeson," and V's identification with Sebastian is implicitly and indirectly hinted at in the doctor's telegram, which spells Sebastian's name in the Russian way— "Se*v*astian's state hopeless come immediately Starov"—and "for some reason unknown" makes V stand for a moment in front of the looking glass (160, emphasis mine). In addition, *The*

Prismatic Bezel abounds in situations where strangers discover that they are related to each other, just as V's quest leads him to discover that Nina Rechnoy and Mme Lecerf are one and the same person.

Success is a novel of quest, with an obvious Percival Q. as the researcher and is analogous to V's quest both in its subject and in its use of false scents and delays.[5] *Success* also contains a series of near meetings between its protagonists, paralleling V's near meeting with the unwitting Clare in the street (65).

The Back of the Moon contains one of Sebastian's liveliest characters, "a meek little man" called Siller, who helps three miserable travelers while waiting for a train (86). He has a bald head, a big strong nose, bushy eyebrows, and a constantly moving Adam's apple (ibid.). The meek and helpful Mr. Siller becomes Mr. Silbermann at the level of V's quest. Like Siller, Silbermann helps a miserable traveler (V) on a train, and like Siller, Silbermann has "a pink bald head" (104), "a big shiny nose" (ibid.), "bushy eyebrows" (103), and an Adam's apple that keeps "rolling up and down" (105). As if to clinch the analogy, Silbermann advises V to stop searching for his brother's fatal woman because one cannot see "de odder side of de moon" (ibid.), reminding us of the story in which his counterpart "makes his bow, with every detail of habit and manner" (86).

In *Lost Property,* Sebastian's most nearly autobiographical novel, the narrator tells the story of a profound experience he had while visiting the small hotel at Roquebrune, where his mother had died. Later, he adds, he mentioned this experience to a relative in London only to learn that he had made a dreadful mistake: "but it was the other Roquebrune, the one in the Var" (17). The experience, nevertheless, was real. V has an analogous "wrong/right" experience when he sits by the bed of a dying man, believing that it is Sebastian (who is already dead) and feeling, as he had never done before, intense affinity with his half brother. This ex-

perience gradually leads V to the climactic recognition of interchangeability and identification.

> So I did not see him after all, or at least I did not see him alive.
> But those few minutes I spent listening to what I thought was
> his breathing changed my life as completely as it would have
> been changed, had Sebastian spoken to me before dying.
> Whatever his secret was, I have learnt one secret too, and
> namely: that the soul is but a manner of being—not a constant
> state—that any soul may be yours, if you find and follow its
> undulations. The hereafter may be the full ability of con-
> sciously living in any chosen soul, in any number of souls, all
> of them unconscious of their interchangeable burden. Thus—I
> am Sebastian Knight. (172)

Sebastian's last novel, *The Doubtful Asphodel,* yields even
more analogies with V's quest. The subject of the novel (as we
have already seen) is a dying man who has a secret, an absolute
truth, to divulge, and who dies before uttering the word that
would have changed the lives of all those who could have ben-
efited from the disclosure. In a similar fashion, V tries desperately
to reach the dying Sebastian in the belief that "he had something
to tell me, something of boundless importance" (162), but
Sebastian dies, and it is too late for the extraordinary revelation
to come from his lips. There is one crucial difference, however, in
V's experience: He does discover a secret—not from Sebastian's
mouth but from the silent breathing of the "wrong Sebastian" in
the wrong room.

Around the central character in *The Doubtful Asphodel* there
are other lives that constitute "but commentaries to the main
subject":

> We follow the gentle old chess player Schwarz, who sits down
> on a chair in a room in a house, to teach an orphan boy the

moves of the knight; we meet the fat Bohemian woman with
that grey streak showing in the fast colour of her cheaply dyed
hair; we listen to a pale wretch noisily denouncing the policy
of oppression to an attentive plainclothes man in an ill-famed
public house. The lovely tall prima donna steps in her haste
into a puddle, and her silver shoes are ruined. An old man sobs
and is soothed by a soft-lipped girl in mourning. Professor
Nussbaum, a Swiss scientist, shoots his young mistress and
himself dead in a hotel room at half past three in the morning.
(147)

Most of these people are analogous, to the point of identity,
with minor characters in V's search. Schwarz, the chess player,
is—with a simple translation of the name—Uncle Black at the
Rechnoy house, and Rechnoy himself opens the door to V, holding "a chess-man—a black knight—in his hand" (118).[6] This is
analogous not only to V's quest but also to Sebastian's life:
Sebastian's name is Knight, and he signed his English poems with
"a little black chess knight drawn in ink" (15). Later in V's quest,
it is again chess that helps him remember the name of Sebastian's
hospital. In the telephone booth "some anonymous artist had be-
gun blacking squares—a chess board, *ein Schachbrett, un damier*
(166), hence St. Damier.

The orphan boy in *The Doubtful Asphodel* parallels the one
who opens the door at Helene Grinstein's, and the "soft-lipped
girl in mourning" (147) is Helene herself (111–12). The "fat Bohemian woman" is Lydia Bohemsky of V's quest, and the "plainclothes man" may again be Silbermann (105). There is no obvious
parallel in V's quest to the man who denounces the policy of oppression. The "lovely prima donna" is analogous to Helene von
Graun, who has "a splendid contralto" (109) and who, like the
prima donna of the novel, steps into a puddle when she arrives at
Mme Lecerf's country house. Finally, the episode of Professor

Nussbaum and his young mistress is similar to the story the hotel manager at Blauberg tells V: "In the hotel round the corner a Swiss couple committed suicide in 1929" (102).[7]

The similarities between *The Doubtful Asphodel* and V's quest are so close to being identical that the distinctions between the levels seem in imminent danger of disappearing. Sebastian's novel almost dictates the development of V's quest. It is not only that the quest has "that special 'Knightian twist' about it," as V puts the idea during his visit to Mme Lecerf (131). The quest is actually made to duplicate Sebastian's novel, manifesting the supremacy of fiction over reality, except, of course, that the reality is also fiction, and the fiction is supposed to yield the "real" life of its protagonist.

Further insight may be gained by locating all these analogies within the intricate layering of narrative levels in *The Real Life of Sebastian Knight*.[8] The layering itself tells us something about the fictionality of reality and the reality of fiction. The extradiegetic level is concerned with V's narration and his thoughts about methods of composition and difficulties involved in writing a biography. The diegetic level consists of V's quest for Sebastian's real life, while Sebastian's biography—emerging as it does from conversations between V and key figures in his half brother's life, as well as from V's own memories—becomes a metadiegetic level, a story within a story. That the "real life" should be a doubly fictional narrative (the novel we read and, to boot, a metadiegetic level in it) may be an initial suggestion of the fictional nature of reality.

There are other metadiegetic levels in addition to Sebastian's life, some taking the form of written documents, some essentially nonverbal but translated into writing. To begin with, there is V's report of Goodman's book, *The Tragedy of Sebastian Knight,* which V demolishes and finally labels *The Farce of Mr. Goodman.* Then there are notes, like Sebastian's last letter to his half brother or Dr. Starov's telegram to V. Among the nonverbal metadiegeses are V's prophetic dream about his half brother and Roy Carswell's portrait of Sebastian.

But this is not all. If Sebastian's life is a metadiegetic level, his novels—often narrated in detail and "quoted from"—constitute a meta-metadiegetic level. And if Sebastian's life is a fiction not to be trusted, Sebastian's fictional works seem closer to his "real life" than his day-to-day reality, as reconstructed through V's conversations with the various informants. But even Sebastian's novels do not really yield the truth for, as Sheldon suggests, "His novels and stories were but bright masks, sly tempters under the pretence of artistic adventure leading him unerringly toward a certain imminent goal" (87). All the authors in Nabokov's novel wear masks. Goodman wears a black one (48, 49, 50), which the narrator pockets in the hope that "it might come in usefully on some other occasion" (50). Sebastian's novels are bright masks, and at the end V realizes that "try as I may, I cannot get out of my part; Sebastian's mask clings to my face, the likeness will not be washed off" (173).[9] As in deconstruction, the real face cannot be seen, behind every mask there is another mask, and there is no way of stopping the interchangeability between reality and fiction.

Within Sebastian's novels there is a further meta-level consisting of letters written by his metadiegetic characters (the love letter and the business letter in *Lost Property*). These are analogous both to Sebastian's life and to V's quest.

The perplexing effect of what Nabokov himself described as a "hell of mirrors" (Nabokov 1967, x) is enhanced by the interpenetration of the various narrative levels. The diegetic V is not only analogous to various elements of the metadiegetic level of Sebastian's life, but is also infused into one of them. The description of Sebastian's last meeting with his first love, as rendered by Natasha Rosanov, unwittingly uses the narrator's name as part of the scenery: "A last change: a V-shaped flight of migrating cranes;

their tender moan melting in a turquoise-blue sky high above a tawny birch-grove" (114–15). A similar use of the name is made in the letter written by the fictional character in Sebastian's *Lost Property:* "Life with you was lovely—and when I say lovely, I mean doves and lilies, and velvet and that soft pink 'v' in the middle" (93).[10] Not only V's initial but also other features of his personality are evoked in this letter by association and analogy. The brokenhearted lover, for example, knows that he will nevertheless "joke with the chaps in the office" (94), and we know that V works in an office. The character in the letter has not been able to bring some business to a satisfactory end (ibid.), and V too is unsuccessful in clinching some bureaucratic matter (151–52).

Lost Property also contains another interpenetration of elements, though these are both at the same level. Of the letters found in the air crash, one is addressed to a woman but begins "Dear Mr. Mortimer," while another is addressed to a firm of traders—and contains a love letter. Not only did the actual letters get confused, but the one contains details from the other, for we read in the love letter: "I have not been able to clinch the business I was supposed to bring 'to a satisfactory close,' as that ass Mortimer says" (94).

V's description of *The Doubtful Asphodel* treats the book and the events narrated in it as if they belonged to the same level: "A man is dying, and he is the hero of the tale; . . . The man is the book; the book itself is heaving and dying, and drawing up a ghostly knee" (147). The intermingling of the book and its narrative reaches a metaphoric climax when the landscape (itself used as a comparison) is described in terms of vowels, consonants, and sentences:

> The answer to all questions of life and death, 'the absolute solution' was written all over the world he [the dying man] had known: it was like a traveller realizing that the wild country he surveys is not an accidental assembly of natural

phenomena, but a page in a book where these mountains and forests, and fields, and rivers are disposed in such a way as to form a coherent sentence; the vowel of a lake fusing with the consonant of a sibilant slope; the windings of a road writing its message in a round hand, as clear as that of one's father; trees conversing in dumb-show, making sense to one who has learnt the gestures of their language.... (150)[11]

Knight's act of narration is also treated as if it were at the same level as the events it narrates, so that the author, his narrator, and his hero are almost fused:

And now we shall know what exactly it is; the word will be uttered—and you, and I, and everyone in the world will slap himself on the forehead: What fools we have been! At this last bend of his book the author seems to pause for a minute, as if he were pondering whether it were wise to let the truth out. He seems to lift his head and to leave the dying man, whose thoughts he was following, and to turn away and to think: Shall we follow him to the end? Shall we whisper the word which will shatter the snug silence of our brains? We shall. We have gone too far as it is, and the word is being already formed, and will come out. And we turn and bend again over a hazy bed, over a grey, floating form—lower and lower.... But that minute of doubt was fatal: the man is dead. (151)

The author's lifting his head seems to be at the same fictional level as the visions of the dying man. It is as if a pause at the level of writing actually causes the death at the level of the events.[12]

A similar collision occurs in *The Real Life of Sebastian Knight* when its characters are treated as real people who can read the novel in which they appear. Thus V says about the Russian lady whose diary he studied: "That she will ever read this book seems wildly improbable" (5). He wishes that the Blauberg hotel manager would "never read these lines" (101), wonders whether he should "send [Silbermann] this work when it is finished" (110), and definitely decides to give Nina a copy (145). From one point of view, these references do not transgress the boundaries between levels, since the book is presented as a biography and the characters as real people. But for the real reader, who stands outside the "game" of narrative levels (to the extent that such an "entity" is still conceivable by this point), the characters—including Sebastian and V—are fictional, and therefore cannot really read the book they hold in their hands.

Behind all these levels, Vladimir Nabokov, the author who invented the novel's other authors, is visibly pulling the strings, suggesting, among other things, that both V and Sebastian may be manifestations of himself. V's epiphany, the identification that opens the quest and closes the novel, is not only "I am Sebastian, or Sebastian is I, " but also "or perhaps we both are someone whom neither of us knows" (172). That this someone is probably the real author is further intimated by a game of letters: v is both the beginning and the end of Vladimir Nabokov, and the s of Sebastian is also the first letter of Sirin, the name by which Nabokov signed his Russian novels. Moreover, Nabokov playfully made Sebastian's life analogous to his own. Both were born in 1899 in St. Petersburg, left Russia in 1919, moved to England, and studied at Cambridge. Like Sebastian's mother, Nabokov's mother used to tie her own wedding ring to her husband's with a black ribbon, and, like Sebastian, Nabokov's first love ended with the bitterness of betrayal. "Sebastian's Russian was better and more natural to him than his English" (71), and Nabokov repeatedly said the same thing about himself. Sebastian wrote his novels under his mother's maiden name (Knight); Nabokov did the same with his Russian novels (Sirin). Many more similarities can be discerned by perusing Nabokov's autobiographical *Speak, Memory,* but these will suffice as indications of the identification of both fictional narrators and objects of narration with the real author.

Narrative levels in the novel collide, intersect, and mirror each other, shattering the illusion of their separateness and, with it, the possibility of distinguishing between fiction and reality. What is consequently destabilized is not only the concept of representation but, more radically, that of reality. "Reality," says Nabokov, "is an infinite succession of levels, levels of perception, of false bottoms, and hence unquenchable, unattainable" (Smith and Nabokov 1962). Compared to *Absalom, Absalom!* Nabokov's *The Real Life of Sebastian Knight* comes closer to the ontological doubt that characterizes postmodernism (see the introduction). Nevertheless, a yearning for reality, for representation, sometimes even for an autonomous self also permeates the novel, and access to the "real" of the title is both ironically subverted and nostalgically sought in this borderline text.

4

Christine Brooke-Rose, *Thru*

"Whoever you invented invented you too"

Unlike *Absalom, Absalom!* and *The Real Life of Sebastian Knight,* which are torn between conflicting views of representation and subjectivity, Christine Brooke-Rose's *Thru* explicitly and playfully opts for a postmodernist position. The novel denies the possibility of distinguishing between language and reality and is skeptical about reality's ontological status: "Language is all we have to apprehend reality, if we must use that term" (64).[1] *Thru* also negates representation ("this being a text not an imitation of life" [79], and "You are mad, all of you. You're talking about all these people as if they really existed" [154]). Instead of a traditional self, it posits an indeterminate flux, "forever undefined, never coinciding with himself" (139), replacing the humanist concept by the relational notion of subject, "since subjects are the space of travelling semes the passage of a transformed decision" (158). The book consistently disconnects utterances from any human source to produce a depersonalized movement "from one disembodied voice to another" (59). This logically leads to "the troubled identity of the narrator" (13), "the disappeared narrator" (164), "the narrator as Zero"

(90). Yet, while denying life to characters, narrators, and authors, it gives life to the very process of narration: "Narration is life and I am Scheherezade" (133).

All of these statements seem to have been drawn from a theoretical study rather than a novel, but this is precisely the point. Self-reflexive and metatextual, *Thru* uses the reader's (or critic's) metalanguage as its own object-language, subverting the distinction between the two. But in addition to these explicit statements, *Thru* also "performs" the destabilization it talks about. In what follows, I will analyze the relations between narration and representation as well as between narration and subjectivity as these emerge from *Thru* both constatively and performatively. I will do this in the full awareness that since the various statements are made by characters in the novel, they are—to a large extent—a part of the novel's "performance," the very distinction between constative and performative being problematized by this text's radical narrative strategies.

Taking advantage of its pedagogical framework, *Thru* explicitly discusses the Platonic conception of mimesis: "For mimesis inevitably produces a double of the thing, the double being nothing a non-being which nevertheless is added to the thing, and therefore not totally devoid of value although, however resembling, never absolutely true. C Plato for yourself" (106; cf. also 143–44).

The absence-side of this doubling is emphasized in the quasi-epigrammatic "If mimesis exists non-being is" (14, 108) as well as by the allusion to both Lacan and Wallace Stevens: "For although every discourse presupposes a blind spot it never the less implies the absence of things as desire implies the absence of its object" (103; cf. also 143).

The reader acutely experiences the absence of things—or at least their undecidability—in a performative repetition, when trying to figure out what happens in *Thru*. As in Escher's painting of two hands, each of which can be seen as drawing the other, so in

Thru what seems to be a narrating subject changes places with what may be understood as a narrated object, collapsing the hierarchy of narrative levels and suggesting that there may be no reality apart from its narration. However, before embarking on an analysis of the reversibility of levels in this text, a preliminary caveat is in order. Although the symmetrical interchangeability of narrator and narrated does indeed exist in _Thru,_ it often disappears into "no narrator at all but a lacuna through which it is possible to fall into delirious discourse" (54). This is governed by "the principle . . . that you don't follow the principle" (76), giving rise to the question repeatedly asked at all levels: "Who speaks?" (1, 22, 35, 42, 59, 89, 107, etc.).

Who, then, speaks in _Thru?_ One could perhaps identify the speaker with the Master, borrowed from Diderot's _Jacques le fataliste_ and functioning here as a kind of dramatized narrator. Although the Master appears only three times in _Thru,_ his conversations with his servant and alter ego, Jacques, concerning the composition of a text occur around the beginning, middle, and end of the novel (16–17, 60–70, 149) and can be understood as representing the overall act of narration. The text they compose is presumably the one we read, since its main characters, like _Thru_'s, are a couple by the names of Larissa Toren and Armel Santores. However, Larissa herself is also in the process of composing a text. "But which text?" asks the Master. "It looks mightily as if she were producing this one" (66). If both Larissa and the Master are said to be writing the text we read, their roles as narrators become interchangeable. Not only does this mean, as the Master jokingly puts it to Jacques, "that the narrator I transformed into Larissa am no longer your master but your mistress" (ibid.). It also means that the object of the Master's narration is transformed into the narrator of the text we read, and possibly becomes the inventor of both Jacques and the Master. No wonder the Master is bewildered and enraged that "this woman Larissa has . . . usurped my place as narrator" (67).

Moreover, in the middle of writing her text, Larissa is interrupted by a visitor called Armel, a friend of her neighbor's, a black writer from Timbuctoo whom she does not know. This Armel gives her naive criticism of her previous book (61–65). Another Armel is Larissa's husband (later ex-husband), and there is an early suggestion, rejected later, that he may be black (46). If the interrupting Armel is identical with the husband, then the scene between him and Larissa is probably a flashback, perhaps their first meeting. Occurring where it does, this scene reinforces the blurring of fictional levels, since Armel, who formerly appeared as a character in the Master's narrative (like Larissa herself), is now promoted to the first degree of fictionality, where he converses with "Larissa Toren, author" (64), who may have invented Jacques and the Master (or rather borrowed them from Diderot) as dramatized narrators for her text. On the other hand, it is also possible that the whole scene between Larissa and Armel is part of the Master's text.

In order to bring the conversation with Armel to a close, Larissa "acquire[s] a sudden husband as a last minute escape" (67). The Master, who makes that comment, is also convinced that "Of course her husband if true would have to be Armel" (ibid.). This is confusing, in view of the fact that she tells Armel about a husband who—according to the Master—must be Armel. So perhaps the two Armels are not the same person: "That's a coincidence," the Master explains at this point to the perplexed Jacques. "They do happen despite the critics" (67).

In addition to the dramatized gentleman narrator, *Thru* is replete with references to "the unomniscient unprivileged unreliable narrator" (32), whom the Master may have created to narrate the story of Armel, Larissa, and the others, but who may also be a narrator above that one, posing the Master and his servant as narrating agencies for his own narrative. Like the dramatized narrator, this disembodied voice is also confusingly equated with Larissa, either through analogies or through explicit identification. The minutes of a staff meeting state, "Larissa Toren is opposed to all horizontal coordination which, according to her, would degenerate into useless chatter" (96); later we hear, "the horizontal coordination degenerates, according to the narrator, into useless chatter" (147). And Armel accuses Larissa of having invented him and withdrawn, "indifferent, paring your fingernails" (25–26), a Joycean attribute of authors often applied in *Thru* to the unreliable narrator (cf. 87). Is Larissa then the narrator in whose narrative she appears as a character? She sometimes considers this possibility: "Whoever invented it is the absent narrator or you in love with the unreliable narrator who is in love with the implied author who is in love with himself and therefore absent in the nature of things" (137–38; see also 96–97).

Whoever the narrator is, one of the objects of his narration is a radical university, with students from all over the world, where Armel and/or Larissa seem to be teaching.[2] This institution of learning is said (by whom?) to have been "dreamt up by the unreliable narrator of the moment who however will be tactfully dropped without scene or motivation" (55). Since that narrator often merges into his dramatized counterparts or into Larissa, she or they could, by the same token, have invented the radical university. But who, in that case, can tactfully drop the unreliable narrator without scene or motivation? If he is himself dreamt up by the dramatized narrator or by Larissa, one of them can obviously drop him. But if he is either equivalent to them or is their creator, who can dispose of him "from above"?

An interesting possibility emerges here, for the academic course the narrative most often focuses on is creative writing, where a collective text rather uncannily similar to *Thru* is being composed. It is quite possible that the class is the collective author, inventing and dropping the unreliable disembodied voice as well as Larissa and the Master as narrators. "After all it's our text, isn't it? for us only," the teacher says (75). But if the class composes the text and sets up its narrators, how can it also be dreamt up by the very narrators it invents? One of the students is disturbingly aware of this double bind: "What are you talking about Ali this is the text we are creating it verbally we are the text we do not exist either we are a pack of lies dreamt up by the unreliable narrator in love with the zeroist author in love with himself but absent in the nature of things, an etherised unauthorised other" (155).

Nor do the complications stop here. The creative writing class is probably taught by Armel, and Larissa's name in the schedule as well as her comments at the staff meetings could be a part of the collective composition or of Armel's own novel. But since Larissa herself also writes a text (*Thru?*), whether she teaches at the same university or at another, it is quite possible that she transforms Armel (and the class) into characters in her novel, or even that she transforms herself into Armel.

Armel and Larissa are both teachers and characters in the collective narrative composed by the creative writing students, making the students' conversation at times particularly perplexing:

> You're mad, all of you. You're talking about all these
> people as if they really existed.
> Oh shut up Ali we're having fun inventing. (154)

As characters in the students' composition, Armel and Larissa do not really exist. As teachers they do exist, but—in another turn of the screw—even as teachers they exist only as fictional characters in *Thru*. Imagine Armel, the teacher, listening to (and perhaps even participating in) the lively exchange among the students about him as a character:

> if it weren't for that illiberal and catastrophic chapter in which
> you re-invented him as an ideal husband, articulate and
> crueltobekind, in order to dialogue lunatically with yourself.
> What do you mean? That was real.
> . . . Already Myra slipped him into the wrong rectangle as a
> black man last term. (150–51)

Or about his ex-wife, Larissa:

So what do you think, should we kill off Larissa?
She sure asks for it. (150)

The collective narrative is not exclusively oral. Some of its sections are submitted by the students as written exercises, but the same interchangeability of levels that governs the oral composition operates here, too. Rather than signaling the nature of such segments in advance, *Thru* first presents them as if they were the narration of primary fictional events (possibly told by the absent or the dramatized narrator). Only later, when we reach the teacher's comments or the class discussion, do we realize that these events are a fiction within a fiction, that is, parts of a student's composition (45–48, 58–59, 71–73). Armel's comments on these written segments reinforce the reversibility of levels, for they could be said of *Thru* with equal justification. "The narrator could in fact disappear entirely though you've woven him in quite well," he writes to one student (48); and to another: "Very good. I like the mixture of levels" (73). Such remarks again promote the students' compositions to the level of the text in which they appear and whose structural principles they share (or create). Armel's comments are written by hand, the handwriting being that of Christine Brooke-Rose, author of *Thru*. This not only reinforces the analogy between *Thru* and the collective composition within it, but also inserts the biographical author—supposedly outside the interchangeability of narrative levels—into the text. The assumption of some inviolate level outside the game is completely undermined, and the author is no longer the origin of the text but one of its effects.

Armel and Larissa, we have seen, play two hierarchically incompatible yet interchangeable roles: They are both university teachers in *Thru* and characters in a collective narrative composed by Armel's students. If we set aside this ambiguity of levels and examine the relations between Armel and Larissa at each level separately (though we can never know which is which), we soon realize that another form of reversible hierarchy is intro-

duced—even when the two should be on a par. This form of hierarchy is realistically motivated both by the kind of people Armel
and Larissa are said to be (both as primary fictional characters
and as inventions in the students' narrative) and by their being
writers who fictionalize each other in their work (again at both
levels).

As a person (that is, as a fictional character at one level or another) Armel can relate to Larissa (and vice versa), only by creating an image of himself—a kind of persona—for her and an image
of her for himself. In his letter to Larissa, Armel asks: "Have you
not carefully invented the person you have become?" (26) and—
at a different narrative level (unless the letter is also part of the
collective composition)—the students ask the same question:
"But Larissa? and our Larissa? Has she not carefully invented the
person she has become?" (151). Armel realizes that he could also
be said to have created Larissa, an invention she fully recipro-
cates: "And perhaps it was after all I who invented you though
you would not admit this. Certainly you invented me and with-
drew" (26). The students also see Larissa—now a character in
their fiction—as creating an image of Armel for herself: "That's
precisely why one has to reinvent him all the time. I mean that's
why Larissa had to" (151). This mutual invention, with a few
more characters added, is tabulated by one of the possible narrators of *Thru* before any of the characters have been properly
"presented":

unless Armel inventing Larissa

or	Larissa	"	Armel
"	Armel	"	Veronica
"	Veronica	"	Armel
"	Armel	"	Larissa
"	Larissa	"	Marco (or is it Oscar?)
"	Marco (?)	"	Larissa
"	Larissa	"	Armel

(8. The table is then repeated in reverse.)

The table is, by its nature, endless: "It follows therefore that if Larissa invents Armel inventing Larissa, Armel also invents Larissa inventing Armel" (108), and so on ad infinitum.

Just as they fictionalize each other in their fictional lives, so they fictionalize each other in their fictional fictions. In what seems like the first tête-à-tête between Armel (future husband or stranger-interrupter?) and Larissa, various elements ("the man from Porlock," the remark about the white lines formed on the black hands, among others) are repeated from the text Larissa composes as he enters. It is as if her text anticipates the "reality" between Armel and herself, just as—according to the students—it does in relation to Stavro, her lover after the separation from Armel: "They'd meet for a drink on the castle terrace [Larissa, Stavro, and his new girlfriend] and Larissa would say tell me how did you two meet closing the manuscript in which she'd be inventing the whole episode before she knew it would turn out that way" (153).

Larissa herself talks to Armel about Stavro both as her lover and as a character in a text she is writing: "That's why I transferred the whole narrative to Rome, the International Theme you know, as well as the psychosis" (132). And just as she (re)invents both Stavro and Armel in her writing, so she encourages Armel to do the same with her: "Write your text and reinvent me in the present tense, which is a convention like any other tense. . . . Whoever you invented invented you too. That surely is the trouble, we do not exist" (53).

Larissa's novels not only transfer her fellow characters to a further degree of fictionality; they also parallel the governing structural principles of *Thru*, in which they are contained. This is particularly evident when Armel (the husband or the other?) criticizes Larissa's book in terms that could apply to *Thru*, and her answers become an inbuilt defense of *Thru*, disarming potential critics in advance. Two examples clarify this point. Armel wonders why the publisher advertises Larissa's book as funny: "Of course it's not funny you are weeping all the time it is one long cry of anguish" (62), and she answers: "So, I'm weeping all the time and yet I'm merely amusing myself. But isn't the only thing to do with a long cry of anguish to amuse oneself? In my country we never separate the two. I take it as a compliment. But you seem to utter these phrases as reproaches" (63). Like Larissa's novel, *Thru* is a combination of witty self-amusement and a cry of anguish, and it is impossible to know whether its author is sad to be glad or glad to be sad—she certainly does not separate the two. Another aspect Armel attacks is the "fall into language": "Why this flight? . . . What I mean is there are moments when you touch on the very essence of things and then brrt! you escape, you run away into language" (62). And Larissa answers—for herself and to all critics of *Thru*—"You mean that when I touch on the essence of things, in that text, it's not by means of language? What is it then?" (ibid.), and "Language is all we have to apprehend reality, if we must use that term" (64).

With this parallel between Larissa's text and *Thru*, we have come full circle to the possibility envisaged at the beginning of this chapter, namely—in the Master's words—"It looks mightily as if she were producing this one and not, as previously appeared, Armel, or Armel disguised as narrator or the narrator I disguised as Armel, That's not clear" (66).[3] It is indeed unclear both because Larissa may be producing this text but may also be invented by its dramatized or undramatized narrator or even by the students' collective composition, and because it deprives the reader of the possibility of distinguishing between narrating subject and narrated object, container and contained, outside and inside, higher and lower narrative levels, plunging him/her into a situation not far from Russell's paradox of "the class of all classes which are not members of themselves." The paradox can be illustrated by the amusing anecdote about the barber who shaves all—but only—only those villagers who cannot shave themselves.

Does the barber, then, shave himself? Either answer produces a contradiction. If he does shave himself, then he can, so disqualifying him from the class of villagers who cannot shave themselves. If, on the other hand, he does not shave himself, then there is one person in the village who cannot shave himself and whom the barber does not shave—which contradicts the premise contained in the first sentence. Russell solved his paradox by the theory of logical types, postulating that a class is of a higher type than its members and should not be confused with them (Russell and Whitehead 1964, 37–66). Thus the barber cannot be used to name both the class and one of its members. This solution is similar to the distinction between metalanguage and object-language, designed to prevent similar paradoxes in language. But the hierarchy that solves Russell's paradox becomes ambiguously reversible in *Thru,* blocking all possible resolution.

The reversibility of hierarchies calls into question the notion of representation. Traditional views of literature as representation assume, in one way or another, a reality (or a fictional reality) that precedes the act of narration of which it is the object (see chapter 1). But transforming the narrated object into the narrating agency, and vice versa, as *Thru* constantly does, not only plunges one into a universe of paradox, infinite regress, and tight loop, but also puts in doubt the separation between reality and narration and questions the very notion of representation.

In dismantling representation, *Thru* displays a wide range of alternatives. As should be clear from the preceding analysis of the process of mutual invention, representation is replaced by presentation, reproduction by production, and re-creation by creation. To clinch the matter, however, let me reiterate a short passage already quoted, which emphasizes both the status of narration as creation and its correlative interrogation of "real existence": "What are you talking about Ali this is the text we are creating it verbally we are the text we do not exist either we are a pack of lies dreamt up by the unreliable narrator in love with the zeroist author in love with himself but absent in the nature of things, an etherised unauthorised other" (155).

"We are the text" recalls such similar expressions as "You are the sentence I write I am the paragraph" (145), foregrounding textuality as another alternative to representation. Textuality is reinforced by many explicit declarations, of which I shall quote only two: "A text is a text is a text," (57) itself an intertextual variation on Gertrude Stein, and "within the grammar of that narrative the roles can be interchanged and textasy multiplied" (87).[4] Textuality is also playfully "performed" by highlighting various aspects of "the materiality of the sign." Acrostics (e.g., 6, 11) and other graphic patterns (e.g., 40, 85) foreground the visual aspect; alliterations and sound repetitions (e.g., the proximity of 'Ruth' and 'Thru' "for mixed reasons of phonemic contiguity" [17]) enrich the acoustic qualities; anagrams and palindromes play with the linear character of language and simultaneously emphasize, on the verbal level, the reversibility of the narrative structure. Larissa uses a near anagram to explain her personality, "I'm rotten through and through you know, my name is Toren" (135).[5] A more complex game describes her relationship with Armel, as mirrored by their names. The inventor and the invention of the other, Armel Santores and Larissa Toren are again near anagrams whose few extra or missing letters foreshadow their incompatibility. Armel's name contains an *m* and an *e,* absent from Larissa's; hers includes an *i* not present in his. "Why ask what went wrong?" Larissa writes to Armel, "you can make up answers such as you didn't find your ME in me or you kept it nor did I find my I in you but kept it" (53; see also 69, where the anagram is explicitly explained). What went wrong in a human relationship is reduced to missing letters in the lovers' names, and the play of language reigns supreme.

Whereas anagrams create a different word by interchanging letters, palindromes are even closer to Escher's drawing hands.

The hands look identical, being in fact reverse images of each other. They interact circularly, so that the right hand can be seen as drawing the left and vice versa. Palindromes are similarly two-directional, producing exactly the same word (or expression) when read forwards or backwards. Wishing to crown Larissa's fictional life with a banal death, the class is engaged in a language game: "What shall we do, kill her off? Eliminate her to Lima or let her die in Rome?" and their decision is a perfect palindrome: "But she must die in ROMA AMOR spelt backwards of course" (152). The two words are reversed mirror images, undermining the order of perception, just as Escher subverted its hierarchy. Appropriately, the text exits with a visual mirroring of its title and a performative declaration of its self-reflexiveness:

reflecting nothing but

T

E

X

(I)

U ЯH T H R U (164)

Textuality in *Thru* is largely a matter of intertextuality, "a text which in effect is a dialogue with all preceding texts" (43; see also 121). My purpose here is to show that intertextuality does indeed become an alternative to representation in *Thru*, not to analyze the numerous allusions and quotations in this text, so I limit my examples to one string of quotations from literary texts and one playful interaction with a seminal theoretical study.[6] Any distinction between the two types is, as I have already suggested, undermined in *Thru*. T. S. Eliot, Shakespeare, E. M. Forster, Dante, and Wallace Stevens meet in the following passage, creating through their contiguity a story of the failure of communication: "And if one settling a pillow by her head should say That is not what I meant at all That is not it at all, fill the air with quotations for the aisle is full of noises where angels fear to tread nel mezzo del cammin because I do not hope to turn again where the lack of imagination had itself to be imagined for a flash of an hour" (44). The second example comes from one of the classroom situations in *Thru*. It begins with the teacher reminding the class, "We must not confuse the levels of discourse . . . I am not a function of your narrative and we are using a metalanguage" (50). This is followed by Jakobson's six functions of language and an appended comment:

> There should be placards saying: Danger. You are now entering the Metalinguistic Zone. All access forbidden except for Prepared Consumers with special permits from the Authorities.
>   M-phatically. (51; see also 126)

The passage above exemplifies not only intertextuality, but also metatextuality, since it becomes an indirect comment on *Thru,* especially by way of contrast. In opposition to the teacher's warning, *Thru* does mix the levels of discourse, as well as the levels of narrative, and placards are precisely what it omits. Placards would operate like Russell's theory of logical types or a clear demarcation between language and metalanguage, but there is no such comfort in *Thru*. In the absence of signposts around its metalinguistic zone, this complex text causes many readers to feel that they are not Prepared Consumers and therefore have little access to it. Larissa and Armel's conversation about language (62–64), quoted earlier, can also be taken as metatextual commentary on *Thru,* on what Armel sees as a flight into language and Larissa as an amused acceptance (even exploitation) of its predominance. In addition to comments on itself, *Thru* is also characterized by metatextual statements about writing in general, as well as by a broader interrogation of the metalanguage of linguistics, literary theory, and psychoanalysis within its own object-language. The result is not only a "delirious discourse" (54) on discourse, but also a transformation of the reader into an element of the text. In this way the reader loses her or his traditionally secure external position.

Thru, I have argued, is predominantly a text about texts. This statement, however, is less one-sided than it may seem, for *Thru* tends to expand the concept of text to make it refer to the whole world. It thus speaks of "a text like the world or the human body" (14–15; see also 55, 106–7) as well as "a text like love" (82; see also 143). If all the world is a text, then the textuality of literature reflects or dramatizes the textuality of the world, and a nonrepresentational text like *Thru* acquires an unexpected representational dimension.

One can detect representation of a more straightforward type in *Thru,* especially when the subject is the frustrating and castrating aspect of love and sex, the double standard and other gender inequalities, illness involving the removal of rotten organs (another form of castration, perhaps), radical universities, or racism.[7] The representational effect of many scenic renderings of these themes is subsequently deconstructed by being revealed as a section from a character's novel, a part of the collective composition, and so on (see, e.g., 45–48). But since the deconstruction is retrospective, a residue of the "realism" of the scene inevitably remains. Some readers may conceive of such glimpses of reality as no more than the bribes of traditional narrative. Others may see them as "touching on the very essence of things" (62), from which the "fall into language" is actually a fear-motivated flight. Still others may contend that, far from being nonrepresentational, the play with language in *Thru* is an attempt to represent the clichéd nature, the inescapable intertextuality, of all expressions of love, racism, and revolutionary ideas. All these are perhaps no more than ideological constructs, discursive practices that govern our existence even though (or because?) they are no more than mystifications masquerading as truths. I point out the possibility of such interpretations in order to reflect on the persistence of representation in some form even in a highly nonrepresentational text. May not this persistence support a view of representation as an effect of the access function of narration in both postmodernist and earlier types of narrative? If such a rehabilitation seems to go against the grain of this text, *Thru* indirectly legitimizes it by saying, "Everything exists even the discourse you do not choose" (153).

As for the status of subjectivity in narration, one of the metatextual passages in *Thru* puts the problem in a nutshell: "which is why modern novels can be so disorientating despite the fact that through this chaotic freedom in the network of possibilities we fill the air with noises, twiddle along the timetable from left to right and back, from one disembodied voice to another. . . . Go forth and multiply the voices until you reach the undeicidable even in some psychoasthmatic amateur castrate who cannot therefore sing the part" (59). *Thru* links narrators with indeterminacy and dissociates voices from any originating self.

Responsible for this dissolution of the traditional link between narration and "self" are various features discussed in the previous section from a different perspective. By turning narrating subjects into narrated (or invented) objects, the reversibility of narrative levels depersonifies narrators, making them into texts, stories, even fictions. And by creating a "confusion of voices" (116) and a quick, often unmarked, transition from one "tale-bearer" to another, the novel seems to answer its recurrent question "who speaks?" in the manner of Barthes: "The discourse, or better, the language, speaks, nothing more" (1974, 41).[8] Finally, the abundant use of intertextuality also contributes to the effacement of the source of utterances, since the voice of the individual is swallowed up in the collective system of cultural discourse.

With a (parodic?) overtone of Marxist slogans and a playful allusion to Lewis Carroll, *Thru* executes the narrator: "There's no more private property in writing, the author is dead, the spokes-

man, the porte-parole, the tale-bearer, off with his head" (29).
But although the narrator is executed, the act of narration itself is
alive and kicking. In class, the teacher develops the hypothesis
that in Homer's period, the community assumes both roles, emit-
ting and receiving a discourse it addresses to itself: "Indeed, the
community is the discourse" (28). The background lecture ends
with an inscription on the board, accompanied by an explanation, and both are applicable in *Thru* far beyond Homer:

> n a r r a t i o n
> you see not narra*tor* for the reasons just given. (28)

Not only does narration supersede the dead narrator; it is also endowed with a life of its own: "Narration is life and I am
Scheherezade" (133). The recurrent Scheherezade motif, however, suggests that some form of life may spill back from the act of
narration to its agent: "Better known and more significant is
Scheherezade, whose very life is to narrate and whose narration
gives her life, with every new character in the same situation, not
a character but a tale-bearer, whose life also depends on his narration generated by the surplus value left over from the previous
tale and itself generating the next" (40). As long as she can tell she
can live, and so she spends her life narrating.

But how does narration's life-giving capacity tally with the
"off with his head" attitude? I suggest that this seeming contradiction is precisely the drama *Thru* enacts: the narrator dies as an
originating self only to give birth to the narrator as a speaking
subject, but the newborn subject is a creature of paper, a signifier
in the symbolic order. Something similar is Lacanically stated in
Thru in relation to characters and authors: "In this way the construction of a character has to pass through a death, necessary to
the structuring of the subject as subject of utterance, and for his
insertion into the circuit of signifiers, I mean the narration. It is
therefore the recipient, you Jacques, or anyone, the other, who
transforms the subject into author, making him pass through this

zero-stage, this negation, this exclusion which is the author" (69). Authors, characters, and narrators are all subject(ed) to narration, or—more broadly—to language. They are dead as selves but alive as subjects. Yet the death of the narrator is "only a manner of speaking since the text has somehow come into existence" (32). And so there must be some originator who is not only an effect of the text or a signifier in the symbolic order (although, as *Thru* also remarks, "In some languages things do themselves"). Even a deconstruction may not be possible without a deconstructor, and the subversion of the traditional self in *Thru* is as paradoxical as de Man's quoted allegory of the key (chapter 1). His final sentence can serve equally well as my conclusion: "This would imply the existence of at least one lock worthy of being raped, the Self as the relentless undoer of selfhood" (de Man 1979, 172).

5

Samuel Beckett, *Company*

"Devised deviser devising it all for company"

Company seems to me Janus-faced, and in the sequence of texts explored here it also faces both ways. On the one hand, its affinities with *Thru* are striking. Like *Thru,* it subverts representation by a reversibility of the hierarchy between narrators and objects of narration, and the sentence that sums up this reversibility in *Thru*—"Whoever you invented invented you too"—has a close parallel in *Company:* "Devised deviser devising it all for company" (46).[1] Similarly, the "disembodied voices" of *Thru* seem to find an echo in *Company*'s pronominal enactment of a Not-I: "The first personal singular and a fortiori plural pronoun had never any place in your vocabulary" (61). On the other hand, as opposed to *Thru,* where the narration may not be associated with any originating consciousness, *Company* finally does come to rest in the mind of the one who is also the many, and the text becomes a dramatization not only of the act of narration but also of a mind narrating or devising. From this quasi-representational perspective, the reversibility of narrative levels enacts different manifestations of the same creative mind, different positions of the mind in relation to itself: the mind talking to itself about itself, occasionally perceiving itself as if from the outside, often imagining—even inventing—its own activity.

Thus perceived, the text becomes a fictional autobiography of a "fabling" subject who "speak[s] of himself as of another." This feature (like the others just mentioned) is double. It points in the direction of a split, dissociated, fragmented subject, showing signs of the alienation dictated by language, even as it suggests a celebration of plurality and a realization that access to one's own story may require a detour via another.

Janus-like, one face of *Company* looks toward *Thru,* toward postmodernism, with its game of reversible levels and disembodied voices, while the other is turned toward novels like *Beloved* where—in a kind of countermovement—the same strategies are used for a tentative retrieval of representation and rehumanization of subjectivity. This doubleness is at least partly enacted by a rupture between the linear unfolding of the text and the various retrospective insights it yields.

The text opens with what sounds like a typical statement made by an extradiegetic narrator: "A voice comes to one in the dark," but this is immediately complicated by the following single-word exhortation: "Imagine." Is "Imagine" a quotation of the voice's appeal to the "one," or is it addressed to the reader by the extradiegetic narrator?[2] This ambiguity establishes from the start a parallel between the position of the one and the reader—two listeners, perhaps also (as it later transpires) two creators (or devisers). The distinction between the narrator's and the voice's language becomes a matter of pronouns. The narrator speaks *about* the one on his back in the third person: "This he can tell by the pressure on his hind parts" (7). The voice speaks *to* him in the second person: "You are on your back in the dark" (ibid.). An uncomfortable feeling of a split is created, but everything still conforms to the rules of grammar and verisimilitude.

The trouble begins on the next page, where "he" no longer seems to be the one on his back in the dark but another: "Use of the second person marks the voice. That of the third that of the cankerous other" (8). Perhaps the "he" used by the extradiegetic narrator refers to someone else, not to the subject in the dark, a "cankerous other" who in turn conjures up the voice that addresses the "one" as "you." In both cases, however, the extradiegetic narrator remains at the top of the pyramid of narrative *instances*. Not for long, though. The activity of devising (by whom?) is soon introduced, giving rise to a dizzying recursive logic that culminates in the possibility of reversing the pyramid: "In another dark or in the same another devising it all for company. . . . Why in another dark or in the same? And whose voice asking this? Who asks, Whose voice asking this? And answers, His soever who devises it all. . . . Who asks in the end, Who asks? . . . The unthinkable last of all. Unnamable. Last person. I. Quick leave him" (22, 24). So perhaps instead of an extradiegetic narrator who devises a subject on his back in the dark and a voice addressing him as "you," or alternatively an extradiegetic narrator who devises "one" and a "cankerous other," who in turn devises a voice that addresses the subject as "you," perhaps "one" is the deviser of all the others. According to this hypothesis, the whole narrative may be invented and told by the "one"—who, apart from the fleeting moment quoted above, consistently avoids the first person—and it is he who devises the extradiegetic narrator, the voice, and the cankerous other. Self-reflexivity renders the confusing situation even more confusing, and this is true for all hypotheses concerning the deviser's identity: "Deviser of the voice and of the hearer and of himself" (26). Whoever the deviser is, he is now said to devise not only the others but also himself.

As the text progresses, more narrative *instances* are introduced, but these can be fairly readily assimilated to those we are already acquainted with. Thus "hearer" (26, 31, etc.) is taken as a synonym for the one on his back in the dark, since he constantly listens to the voice. "Creature" (26) refers to the same "one," and by implication the "creator," who may be "in the same dark as his creature or in another" (ibid.), is identical with the "he" or the "cankerous other" (see also 51–52). The introduction of the devised deviser, however, destabilizes these smooth equations: "Devised deviser devising it all for company" (46). If there is a devised deviser, there must also be a devising deviser, but who is who, and how can we know? A plausible hypothesis would be that the devising deviser is the extradiegetic narrator (some would prefer to say Beckett). He invents the devised deviser, about whom he speaks in the third person, and who is identical with the cankerous other and the creator. This creator in turn devises the creature who is also the hearer and the one on his back in the dark, who is addressed in the second person by a voice that the creator also invents. With an additional turn of the screw, the creator devises not only the others but also himself—all for company. Plausible indeed, except that earlier suggestions prevent this hypothesis from becoming definitive, and future developments, beginning with the gradual fusion of creator and creature and ending with the concluding lines, completely reverse it.

Analogies between the creator and the creature begin to suggest themselves with the image of the beeline. The creature's walk is described in the "you" mode as follows: "You take the course you always take which is a beeline for the gap or ragged point in the quickset that forms the western fringe" (35–36; see also 38). This image is later transferred to the creator's crawl, described in the "he" mode: "So he crawls the mute count. . . . In what he wills a beeline. . . . In what he hopes a beeline" (49). The analogies fuse as *Company* draws to a close. Segal (forthcoming) convincingly shows that, in the final section, the you mode modulates from addressing the subject on his back in the dark to addressing his fabling creator. As Segal points out, the creator's physical position gradually merges with that of his creature. After his fall, the crawling creator lies prone, flat on his face. The final section, however, traces his gradual transition from a prone to a supine position: "Supine now you resume your fable where the act of lying cut it short. And persist till the converse operation cuts it short again. . . . Till from the occasional relief it was supineness becomes habitual and finally the rule" (62). The uncanny process of fusion culminates in the concluding statement: "Till finally you hear how words are coming to an end. With every inane word a little nearer to the last. And how the fable too. The fable of one with you in the dark. The fable of one fabling with you in the dark. And how better in the end labour lost and silence. And you as you always were. Alone" (62–63). It now seems that the devising deviser is the creature, who is also the hearer and the one on his back in the dark. It is he who has invented the creator (the cankerous other) as a devised deviser, as well as the voice and himself. If so, narrator, narrated, and narratee are the same, and we are back with the "one" of the opening sentence. The text becomes a fictional autobiography that carefully avoids the first person. Why is the "I" eschewed, and why does the narrator speak "of himself as of another"?

As we have seen, narration in _Company_ alternates between sections in the third person and sections in the second. The second-person sections are spoken by a voice and concern partly the present situation of the solitary subject ("You are on your back in the dark") and partly memories, which the voice wishes to convince the one are his (annoying his mother by a comment about the distance of the sky, being encouraged by his father to jump into the water, unwittingly causing the death of a hedgehog, having an ambivalent relationship with a woman). The third-person sections are partly about the one on his back in the dark and partly about an amazingly cerebral creative process—with its hypotheses, hesitations, and reservations—of someone who "devise[s] it all for company" (8). The sections with "you" have an immediate, straightforward, sometimes lyrical effect, whereas those with "he" operate as a skeptical questioning of the authority of the other voice's presentation of experience (Jewinski 1990, 147). The logic behind these shifts, as well as the omission they signal, are a performance, not only a reflection of/upon the conjunction between a "subject without self"[3] and the subjecting aspect of language. The absence of self is explicitly stated in a fleeting paragraph very early in *Company:* "Use of the second person marks the voice. That of the third that cankerous other. Could he speak to and of whom the voice speaks there would be a first. But he cannot. He shall not. You cannot. You shall not" (8). The subject, it transpires, cannot speak in the first person because the first person would be taken as a sign (or illusion?) of self, which is precisely what this subject does not have—he is, one might say, an *être manqué.* As later, in *Beloved,* the non-crystallization of identity is manifested in a fragmentation of the subject, whose objective correlatives are a dismembering of the body, a dissociation from memories, and a fragmentation of the text. In *Company,* the subject is split into different ways of relating to himself. The body is reduced to a back, a hand, an eye, a knee, feet—all disconnected from each other—and the text is fragmented by the alternating pronominal sections.

Fragmentation also takes the form of a discontinuity between the subject's present and his past. On this reading, which is not the only possible interpretation, the achievement of the subject's personal integration is the aim of the deviser: "To have the hearer have a past and acknowledge it. You were born on an Easter Friday after long labour. Yes I remember" (34). By owning one's memories and establishing continuity with the past, one can gain access to a voice and an I: "Another trait its repetitiousness. Repeatedly with only minor variants the same bygone. As if willing him by this dint to make it his. To confess, Yes I remember. Perhaps even to have a voice. To murmur, Yes I remember" (16). But the subject is incapable, or unwilling, to own his memories, hence disclaiming the right to an I as well as to a voice that would speak instead of passively being spoken to and about by other voices. The activity of remembering is not only an act of integration, but also a creation of discontinuity: "Remembering is not simply recuperative. It involves processes of cutting and editing. To re-member is also to dismember" (Arthur 1987, 142).

The incapacity, or refusal, to claim ownership of himself may also explain the use of the third person as a dissociative evasion of responsibility: "He speaks of himself as of another. He says speaking of himself, He speaks of himself as of another" (26). In a similar rejection of the I, the "Unnamable" paradoxically says: "I shall not say I again, ever again, it's too farcical. I shall put in its place, whenever I hear it, the third person, if I think of it. Any-thing to please them. It will make no difference. Where I am there is no one but me, who am not" (355).[4] This passage suggests that being a subject without self is not only an existential predicament but also a consequence of language. "It's the fault of the pro-nouns," says the Unnamable (404), and indeed how can personal pronouns designate specific individuals when, by definition, they are applicable to all individuals (see also Thiher 1984, 132)? In *Company,* such an uncomfortable insight affects not only the use of "I," but also that of "you" and "he," shifters whose reference to the subject cannot be guaranteed: "He cannot but sometimes wonder if it is indeed to and of him the voice is speaking. May not there be another with him in the dark to and of whom the voice is speaking? Is he not perhaps overhearing a communication not in-tended for him?" (8–9). In more general terms, self-alienation is a necessary result of the subject's entry into language, where "I" is always translated by something other than itself. "If the voice is not speaking to him it must be speaking to another. So with what reason remains he reasons. To another of that other. Or of him. Or of another still. To another of that other or of him or of an-other still" (11).

The splitting of the subject, enacted by the interplay of pro-nouns, is doubled, perhaps even parodied, by the use of initials, another substitute for naming. Evoking the divine fiat, the creator muses: "Let the hearer be named H. Aspirate. Haitch. You Haitch are on your back in the dark. And let him know his name" (31).

An initial, of course, is not exactly a name, but—in addition to evoking the sound of breathing, often referred to in the text—*H* is the first letter of both *hearer* and *he,* thus gaining a certain degree of substantiality. But this is only to be immediately dispelled: "Is it desirable? No. Would he gain thereby in companionability? No. Then let him not be named H. Let him be again as he was. The hearer. Unnamable. You" (32). But the game of letters does not stop here. A few pages later, "Feeling the need for company again he tells himself to call the hearer M at least. For readier reference. Himself some other character. W" (42–43). This time the initial confers an even greater substantiality (M = AM), but it also hints at the interchangeability of the two subjects, both by calling the other "AM" and by using two letters that visually mirror each other (M and W). Moreover, W = "double you" (and the hearer was constantly addressed as "you"), thus reinforcing the doppelgänger motif.[5] And M brings to mind Malone and Molloy of the trilogy, intertextual references within the Beckett corpus, which—together with "the Unnamable" and the crawling creature of *How It Is*—may suggest an autobiographical dimension that is not confined to the fictional. In a similar vein, Booth says: "The masterstroke here, for me, is Beckett's reiterated invitation to think about a struggling and suffering someone beyond or behind the three 'characters,' not just the 'cankerous other' who uses the third-person but the implied author himself or even the career-author: Samuel Beckett, telling us once again 'how it is'" (1983, 453). In typical fashion, however, all this is soon undone: "Is there anything to add to this esquisse? His unnamability. Even M must go. So W reminds himself of his creature as so far created. W? But W too is creature. Figment" (45).

My intuition that the use of initials may be parodying the use of pronouns is based on the initials' relatively exaggerated, cruder, less sophisticated nature. The game of initials lays bare the interplay of pronouns, with a characteristically double-edged effect, simultaneously undermining the seriousness of the latter and arming it against irony by dint of an inbuilt parody.

Up to now I have stressed the reductive, dehumanizing effect of the undoing of the traditional self. *Company,* however, is more complex. Even within the deconstructionist framework, this undoing can be seen as a celebration of plurality and freedom. What Carla Locatelli describes as the lack of coincidence of the self with himself gives rise to the plurality of the subject: "In this way, the narrative reflects a conception of the subject that is essentially 'plural' and not immediate, while narration also conveys the notion that this phenomenological 'plurality' would be obliterated in the figure of a singular pronoun" (1990, 160). One can see the lack of unity that defines the traditional self as a multiplicity of roles, characterizing a subject free from the traps of rigidifying conceptualizations in both language and philosophy. And the discontinuity between present and past can be interpreted as a liberation from a pseudo-sameness. Thus, what was earlier interpreted as the subject's disowning of his past memories can be reconceived as an emphasis on the independence of separate periods or moments. When the subject is imagined as acknowledging his memories, he also insists on the pastness of the past, on its non-unity with the present: "One day! In the end. In the end you will utter again. Yes I remember. That was I. That was I *then*" (21; emphasis mine).[6]

In this light, my earlier stress on the subject's disowning of his past memories is open to question. What if these are not his memories at all, but stories the deviser invents and imposes on the subject? After all, the opening page of *Company* says: "To one on his back in the dark a voice tells of a past," not specifying whose past. The deviser's desire that the subject acknowledge the memory of his own birth (34) reinforces such a suspicion. How can anyone remember his or her own birth? Do not such memories always come from the other? Are they not—in fact—memories of the other?

Just as liberation from the chains of time may come at the expense of discontinuity, so can company become the other side of fragmentation. As long as there is unity, there is no company.

Otherness is a necessary condition for company, and when "one" is alone, otherness takes the form of otherness-to-self, namely, split, fragmentation, turning parts or aspects of the subject into separate entities. For example, "Little by little as he lies the craving for company revives. . . . The need to hear that voice again" (55), or "Might not the voice be improved? Made more companionable?" (34), or yet again: "If he were to utter after all? However feebly. What an addition to company that would be!" (21). Similar questions are asked about the hearer—"Might not the hearer be improved? Made more companionable if not downright human"—and, as we have already seen, about the initials considered as possible substitutes for both hearer and subject (32, 42). In the same half-serious, half-ironic tone, parts of the body (e.g., the ear [34]) as well as physical postures (being prone or supine [26–27, 56]) and sensations (an "unscratchable itch" [55]; the smell of the creator [52]; or the sound of the crawl [50]) are said to be an addition to company. Emotional states, such as confusion (26), sickness of the heart (ibid.), and "a movement of sustained sorrow or desire or remorse" (45), also become sociable entities, as do the darkness (26–27) and some hypothetical creatures that would have been welcome in the empty room (a dead rat [27]; a fly [28]). Although not explicitly designated as company, intertextuality clearly functions as such, the voices of Dante, Shakespeare, Milton, and other past authors populating the text through many direct and indirect allusions (Brater 1983, 157–71; Pilling 1982, 127–31).

"In order to be company," says Beckett's text about the one on his back in the dark, "he must display a certain mental activity" (9), and the main activity displayed is—circularly—one of "devising it all for company" (8, 24, 26, 27, 33, 43, 46, 60). The act of devising or creating others for the sake of company is reminiscent of Genesis 2:18: "It is not good that man should be alone; I will make him a helpmeet for him" (King James Version). The biblical "helpmeet" can be reformulated as "companion," and the naming of figment-companions by Beckett's character recalls Adam's naming of the creatures. In association with the intertextual-autobiographical allusions mentioned earlier, a possible analogy emerges between artistic creation and the creation of the world.

Yet *Company* is not only a self-reflexive text about fiction writing. It is also about Everyman, imagining a world, devising company, narrating his own story to himself by inventing others who both are and are not himself. This indirect way of gaining access to oneself is reminiscent of the acts of narration in both *Absalom, Absalom!* and *The Real Life of Sebastian Knight.* In *Absalom, Absalom!* the construction of subjectivity passes through the other in two complementary ways, which I have already formulated semi-epigrammatically: You are what others say about you, and conversely, you are what you say (performatively) about others. In *The Real Life of Sebastian Knight,* whether taken as V's narration or as Sebastian's, the subject gains access to his own story through another's. In *Company* too, it is by telling about "others" that the subject gains access to his own story and his own subjectivity. Otherness is necessary not only for the constitution of subjectivity through narration but for the very existence of a narrative situation. Narration is impossible without a narratee (a "hearer"), and when one is alone, as in *Company,* it is the self-as-other that one addresses. Without company, even the company of projected figments, there is no narration. Therefore the realization that "you [are] as you always were / Alone" ends the text and ends the narration. But the converse is also true: without narration there is no company. In the fashion of *A Thousand and One Nights,* as long as there is storytelling, life and others exist. Once "you hear how the words are coming to an end. . . . And how the fable too," company is over, and you are alone and expiring.

6

Toni Morrison, *Beloved*

"It was not a story to pass on"

Beloved is no less obsessed with narratives and narration than are the other novels analyzed in my study. It poignantly dramatizes a tension between the blocking of story-telling and its eruption, exploring the access potential of narration in recovering the repressed past, retrieving memory, and fighting the suppression of individual and communal voice.

Nor is *Beloved* naive about the possibility of representation. On the contrary, it is as fully aware as the other novels of the problematic nature of stories based on previous stories, themselves deriving from still earlier stories, as well as of the elements of creation and fictionality which necessarily characterize any attempt to recover a past.[1] Similarly, the novel is painfully conscious that subjectivity is fragile in general and becomes even more so under the cruel conditions of slavery. Out of this predicament (and because of it?), however, *Beloved* attempts a hesitant rehabilitation of representation and subjectivity via narration. Indeed, it does not try only to rehabilitate subjectivity, but to go beyond it. From the position of subjects, in the ruthless and racial sense of being "in subjection," the characters yearn for what the novel—in a deliberate approximation to the humanist view—calls a "self." Whereas *Thru* and *Company,* each in its own way, moved from self to subject, *Beloved* dramatizes subjects in search of selves.[2]

In this complex attempt at a retrieval that incorporates destabilizing insights, *Beloved* employs many modernist and postmodernist techniques of narration for purposes different from theirs.[3] As we have seen, the multiplication of narrative levels often enacts a doubt about the possibility of reaching reality and constituting a self. But in *Beloved* the multiplication of levels (and near levels) operates instead as an access to self.[4] Similarly, ambiguity, the genre of the fantastic, and magical realism are often employed in modernist and postmodernist novels for nonrepresentational, self-reflexive purposes. By contrast, in *Beloved* these strategies are subordinate to the attempt (and the difficulty) of making believable the unbelievable horrors of slavery, of trying to represent an unbearable reality.

The endeavor to regain previously dismantled possibilities is not a return to a position before doubt but rather an inclusion of the destabilization and an attempt to transcend it. To support this claim, let me begin by showing how the use of narrative levels both subverts a certain relationship between narrating voice and person, and very subtly suggests that narration may become a basis for a birth into self.

Beloved is related by an extradiegetic narrator who, on the whole, delegates the role of focalizers—and sometimes also of second-degree narrators—to various characters in the novel. Characters seem to become first-degree narrators only in the three interior monologues that follow the discovery of Beloved's identity and culminate in a kind of chorus, fusing Sethe's, Denver's, and Beloved's voices in a ritual-like unification (200–217). These four chapters can support the interpretation that it is the discovery of the other—as well as the experience of loving the other—that endows Sethe, Denver, and Beloved with a voice (I) and a self. But the monologues often convey experiences denying the self (e.g., Beloved's incapacity to dissociate herself from Sethe) or undermining the love (e.g., Denver's suspicion that Sethe might kill her the way she killed Beloved). And the fusion anticipated by the chorus of the three voices turns out to be a debilitating *folie à trois* from which only Denver successfully extricates herself. Moreover, the possibility of an affinity between saying "I" and having an I is probably illusory, even on the grounds of narrative strategies. Bearing in mind the end of the preceding chapter of the novel, one realizes that the monologues may be conceived of as quotations by the extradiegetic narrator, rather than autonomous as they seem to be.[5] True, there are no quotation marks, which is misleading at first—but the last sentence before the monologues is: "Mixed in with the voices surrounding the house, recognizable but undecipherable to Stamp Paid, were the thoughts of the women of 124, unspeakable thoughts, unspoken" (199; end of chapter). The monologues, we now realize, can be seen as the narrator's verbalization of the characters' unspeakable and un-spoken thoughts. Thus there is no easy and direct connection be-tween narration and originating self in *Beloved*.

Despite the lack of a direct connection, however, the novel does assign narration a crucial role in the constitution of self—but indirectly, through a network of narrative levels. Within this net-work, I shall focus on a few scenes whose subject is birth and re-birth, because the association between access to self and birth clearly suggests a stance that goes beyond the problem of subjec-tivity. Furthermore, the conjunction between birth and rebirth metaphors and the presence or absence of narrative levels gives rise to a differentiation between characters who gain access to a self and those who do not, a differentiation that—not surprisingly at this point—hinges on the role of storytelling.

There is an intriguing chiasmus between the narration of birth and of rebirth in *Beloved*. The birth is Denver's; the rebirth, Beloved's. Contrary to expectation, birth, a primary, originary event, is rendered through layers of storytelling, while rebirth, a second coming, is accorded primary narration. By pursuing the unfolding of this paradox and trying to interpret it, we may, I hope, glimpse the relation suggested between narration and self.

Denver's birth is told twice, and it is a highly dramatic event. Sethe is all alone in the woods, running away from Sweet Home, where her back was cruelly pulped and her milk taken away from her in a rapelike scene performed by two whiteboys. Her legs are swollen, she can hardly walk, and she is terrified by a premonition that either she or the baby or both are about to die. Then, with the help of a whitegirl, she reaches a lean-to and later a boat on the river, where her water breaks—as if to join the water of the river. Denver is born there and is named after the whitegirl. This dramatic event also seems to take the dramatic form of a scene. It is presented in great detail, with many dialogues between Sethe and the whitegirl, creating an effect of vividness and immediacy.[6] So strong is the sense of immediacy that the reader often experiences the scenes as a "first narrative"[7] told directly by the extradiegetic narrator, who seems to be quoting the dialogues. The reader thus forgets the multilayered distancing through which the scenes reach him or her. But distancing is prevalent both in the temporal organization and in the handling of narration and focalization in the two renderings of Denver's birth.

The first birth chapter (28–42), although seemingly part of the narrative present, is in fact doubly analeptic. It starts as a flashback, an iterative summary of Denver's secret feasts in her secluded bower in the woods. The iterative gives way to the singulative, and one intimate scene in the boxwood is narrated in which Denver finds herself in snow and then returns home to experience a vision of her mother praying while a white dress kneels next to her in a gesture of tender embrace. Both the snow and the kneeling dress evoke memories in Denver: "And it was the tender embrace of the dress sleeve that made Denver remember the details of her birth—that and the thin, whipping snow she was

standing in, like the fruit of common flowers" (29). The birth
event, then, is an analepsis within an analepsis, doubly distanced
from the narrative present, which deals with the union between
Sethe and Paul D.

A similar distancing occurs in the handling of narration and focalization. Although the chapter is told by the extradiegetic narrator, the narration of Denver's birth is filtered through Denver.
It is Denver who remembers the scene, and through her memories
(verbalized by the narrator) the reader experiences it. But what
Denver remembers is not the event itself but stories Sethe used to
tell her about her birth: "a thin and whipping snow very like *the
picture her mother had painted* as she described the circumstances
of Denver's birth in a canoe straddled by a whitegirl for whom she
was named" (29; emphasis mine). The birth scene is a memory of
a story, and the narrator often reminds us of this by using such expressions as "Sethe told Denver" or by referring to Denver in the
third person: "And now the part that Denver loved the best."[8]

The first birth chapter is told by the extradiegetic narrator, although the narration is filtered through Denver's memories of
stories she has heard. In the second chapter (74–85), however,
even the narration is not primary. The birth events are told (and
focalized) by Denver, an intradiegetic narrator whose narrative
becomes metadiegetic. "'Tell me,' Beloved said. 'Tell me how
Sethe made you in the boat'" (76), and Denver tells. Her narrative
is further distanced by being constructed "out of the strings she
had heard all her life" (ibid.). Denver constantly reminds us of
this by acknowledging Sethe as her source: "The whitegirl, she
said, had thin little arms but good hands. She saw that right away,
she said" (76); "she cried, she said, from how it hurt" (77). The
similarity between this technique and the attribution of stories to
their original tellers in Faulkner's *Absalom, Absalom!* is striking.
Let me recall only two examples out of many. Mr. Compson tells
Quentin: "I have this from something your grandfather let drop
one day and which he doubtless had from Sutpen himself in the

same accidental fashion" (49). Shreve, who hears the story only from Quentin, constructs parts of it with him and says: "And yet, this old gal, this Aunt Rosa, told you that someone was hiding there" (216).

The birth chapters _seem_ like scenes because of the abundance of detail and dialogue, producing an effect of vividness and immediacy, but they are distanced in time, narration, and focalization. Strangely enough, however, the distancing does not make the scenes lose their scenic character, but transposes the scenic quality from the birth event itself to its reliving in the present. In the first birth chapter Denver not only _remembers_ stories she heard about her birth, but "easily she _stepped into_ the told story that lay before her eyes on the path she followed away from the window" (29; emphasis mine). Here Denver "sees" her pregnant mother "walking on two feet meant for standing still" (ibid.), just as in the second birth chapter "Denver began to see what she was saying and not just to hear it: there is this nineteen-year-old slave girl—a year older than herself" (77).[9] Like Quentin and Shreve in _Absalom, Absalom!_ reenacting the Sutpen saga in the present of their own lives, Denver relives her birth as an event in the present: "Denver was seeing it now and feeling it—through Beloved. Feeling how it must have felt to her mother. Seeing how it must have looked" (78).

The complex oscillation between immediacy and distancing is very different from the effect produced by Beloved's reappearance, an uncanny event cast in terms of a rebirth and inviting comparison with Denver's birth. Denver's birth is rendered in great detail, but nothing is said about Beloved's. It is Beloved's return, not her original coming, that the novel dramatizes. This "miraculous resurrection" (105) is associated at the time with Sethe's full bladder: "And, for some reason she could not immediately account for, the moment she got close enough to see the face, Sethe's bladder filled to capacity" (51). At first this may seem only an indication of excitement (or perhaps even a vague recognition of Beloved), but the association with birth-giving becomes gradually stronger as the text unfolds: "The water she voided was endless," and "there was no stopping water breaking from a breaking womb and there was no stopping now" (ibid.). The association between voiding water and giving birth becomes even more specific as Sethe compares her reaction to the unknown/half-known figure of Beloved with her experience of giving birth to Denver: "But as it went on and on she thought, No, more like flooding the boat when Denver was born" (ibid.), an analogy reinforced by Sethe's recollection at this point of a brief exchange between her and Amy, the whitegirl, during the delivery. In both scenes, water is not only evacuated but also imbibed in great quantities. Beloved drinks cup after cup (ibid.), and Sethe drinks and asks for more following Denver's birth (90).[10] The returning Beloved has soft, smooth skin, like a newborn baby (50, 52). In a further analogy between the scenes, Beloved's return becomes a realization of a figurative expression used by Amy. While massaging Sethe's swollen feet, Amy warns her: "It's gonna hurt, now. . . . Anything dead coming back to life hurts" (35; see also 77, 78). Denver, remembering this part of the story, silently comments: "A truth for all times" (35). What is Beloved's return if not a "living" example of something dead coming back to life? And isn't "hurt" both an intransitive and a transitive verb, just as the returning Beloved hurts both herself and others?[11]

The analogy with Denver's birth suggests that Beloved's return is indeed a rebirth. This return "in the flesh," however, is itself a repetition of Beloved's earlier haunting of 124 as a ghost, so that her second coming becomes a third coming. Note how this nonprimary event is narrated: "A fully dressed woman walked out of the water. She barely gained the dry bank of the stream before she sat down and leaned against a mulberry tree. . . . Nobody saw her emerge or came accidentally by" (51). If nobody saw her emerge, the only possible focalizer and narrator of her return is the extradiegetic narrator, and this remains the telling voice throughout the chapter, although focalization is sometimes delegated to characters.

This brings me back to my original perplexity concerning the birth and rebirth scenes: Why is a nonprimary event accorded primary narration, whereas the originary event of Denver's birth is rendered through layers of storytelling? The narrator makes this statement about Sethe's awareness of the meaning of freedom: "Freeing yourself was one thing; claiming ownership of that freed self was another" (95). By analogy, one might say that being born is one thing; claiming ownership of one's birth is another. It is through memory (as focalizer) and storytelling (as narrator) that Denver claims ownership of her own birth and gains access to a self. The reawakening of memory is particularly important in the light of its repression in Denver's childhood. Early in her life, one of the boys at Lady Jones's asks Denver a question about Sethe's murder of Beloved. This question puts an end to Denver's social life, to her reading lessons, to her capacity to hear. Deafness is Denver's defense against unacceptable knowledge. But knowledge, and memory, are necessary for the constitution of personal history, and Denver gradually begins to show an interest in the past, at least in that portion which relates to her own origin. Since she cannot remember her own birth, Denver must cease to be deaf and begin to listen, as she constructs her own history through stories she hears from Sethe: "Denver hated the stories her mother told that did not concern herself, which is why Amy was all she ever asked about" (62).[12] Denver rehearses the memories in her mind as she constructs, rather than reconstructs, a coherent pattern out of "the strings she had heard all her life" (176). However, to be fully creative, narration to the self has to be complemented by narration to the other. When telling the story of her birth to Beloved, Denver gives "blood to the scraps her mother and grandmother had told her—and a heartbeat" (78). Thus, narration becomes most strongly a creation, and most strongly a way of claiming ownership of the self, when the construction is shared: "The monologue became, in fact, a duet as they lay down together, Denver nursing Beloved's interest like a lover whose pleasure was to overfeed the loved . . . and the two did the best they could to create what really happened, how it really was, something only Sethe knew because she alone had the mind for it and the time afterward to shape it" (ibid.).[13]

The layering of focalization and narration in the birth scenes is necessary because it is through memory and storytelling that the fact of birth is transformed into a claiming of ownership and a birth into a self. Toward the end of the novel, Denver's accession to a self is explicitly formulated: "It was a new thought, having a self to look out for and preserve" (252).

Recast in the negative, the foregoing statements can also explain the primary narration of Beloved's return. Beloved's rebirth is not rendered through her memories (as focalizer) or her retrospective telling (as second-degree narrator), because these would have constituted her self, and Beloved does not have a self. But as psychoanalysis has taught us, her incapacity to remember the event causes her to reenact it unconsciously, to return to the world from which she was expelled as a baby.

Let us examine these hypotheses a little further. Although Beloved enjoys listening to stories, much more so than does Denver (see, e.g., 58), she cannot use them to construct a personal history because she has no memory. Indeed, Sethe believes that "Beloved had been locked up by some whiteman for his own purposes, and never let out the door. That she must have escaped to a bridge or someplace and rinsed the rest out of her mind" (119). To be sure, not everything is rinsed out of Beloved's mind: Sethe, and her earrings, are very much there, as is the scene of separation, and the boat full of half dead, half dying slaves, from which her mother escaped into the water. If I may phrase the point somewhat paradoxically, the problem is not that Beloved does not remember the past, but that she does not remember it *as a past:* "it is always now   there will never be a time when I am not crouching and watching others who are crouching too   I am always crouching . . . it is the crouching that is now always now" (210–11). Such an obliteration of temporality negates (personal) history and memory as memory.[14] "Those who cannot remember their past," says Santayana, "are condemned to re-live it." And Beloved relives her past by returning, by being reborn into the world, but not into a substantial self.

Beloved's lack of self has an objective correlative in physical fragmentation. On losing a tooth, she thinks:

> This is it. Next would be her arm, her hand, a toe. Pieces of her would drop maybe one at a time, maybe all at once. Or one of those mornings before Denver woke and after Sethe left she would fly apart. It is difficult keeping her head on her neck, her legs attached to her hips when she is by herself. Among the things she could not remember was when she first knew that she could wake up one day and find herself in pieces. She had two dreams: exploding and being swallowed. When her tooth came out—an odd fragment, last in the row—she thought it was starting. (133)[15]

This experience of the "body in pieces"[16] is the inverse of the association established elsewhere in the novel between an integration of parts and a claiming of the self. When Baby Suggs discovers her freedom, for example, she also discovers that parts of her body cohere into a whole—the whole being her newborn free self: "But suddenly she saw her hands and thought with a clarity as simple as it was dazzling, 'These hands belong to me. These my hands.' Next she felt a knocking in her chest and discovered something else new: her own heartbeat. Had it been there all along? This pounding thing" (141). Sethe similarly links the stirring of memory (in spite of its painful aspects) with a regaining of the body: "Paul D dug it up, gave her back her body, kissed her divided back, stirred her rememory, and brought her more news" (189). And the connection between such integration and love is also emphasized by Paul's memory of Sixo's attitude toward the Thirty-Mile Woman: "She is a friend of my mind. She gather me, man, the pieces I am, she gather them and give them back to me in all the right order. It's good, you know, when you got a woman who is a friend of your mind" (272–73).[17] While remembering the past is associated with re-membering the body, its disremembering is mirrored by physical dismembering.[18]

An additional aspect of an unintegrated self is the lack of dissociation between it and an other.[19] Beloved experiences herself as indistinct from Sethe: "I am not separate from her   there is no place where I stop   her face is my own and I want to be there in the place where her face is and to be looking at it too" (210). The fusion is often reenacted by the pronouns "my" and "mine" in expressions like "my face" or "the face which is mine," which in the context can mean at least three things: her face, which resembles mine; her face, which belongs to me, since she is my mother; my face, which is on her shoulders. The following is one example of many:

> I drop the food and break into pieces   she took my face away
>   there is no one to want me   to say my name . . .
>   . . . I see her face which is mine . . . I have to have my face . . .
> I follow her   we are in the diamonds which are her earrings
> now   my face is coming   I have to have it   I am looking for
> the join . . . now I am her face   my own face has left me . . . I
> want to be the two of us . . . I want the join. (212–13)[20]

Note the association between fusion and fragmentation. Since for Beloved, she and Sethe are one, her mother's disappearance leaves her without her own face. Looking for the join is therefore both a desire to integrate fragmented parts of herself and a longing to reunite with Sethe, a reunion that culminates in expressions like "You are my face, you are me" (216); "Why did you leave me who am you" (ibid.); or "Will we smile at me?" (ibid.). A self that is totally dependent on fusion with another is neither a distinct unit (a self of one's own) nor a unified whole (an unfragmented self, or in-dividuum). In short, it is not really a self.

At the end of the novel, Beloved, who could not remember, is disremembered by others (as well as dismembered); she who had a claim, but could not claim herself, is unclaimed by anyone, and all traces of her disappear into the weather: "Everybody knew what she was called, but nobody anywhere knew her name. Disremembered and unaccounted for, she cannot be lost because no one is looking for her, and even if they were, how can they call her if they don't know her name? Although she has a claim, she is not claimed. In the place where long grass opens, the girl who waited to be loved and cry shame erupts into her separate parts, to make it easy for the chewing laughter to swallow her all away" (274). Beloved is swallowed away. And her story? Her own story she could not narrate, but even stories made up about her cease after a while. A story of one who is reborn without ever being born into a self is as insubstantial as the creature who "wander[s] out of the yard just the way she wandered in" (67).

Some might object that I make too much of Beloved's insubstantiality, which could be seen as part and parcel of her supernatural mode of existence instead of as an indication of her incapacity to gain access to a self. Indeed, my whole comparison between Denver and Beloved might be questioned on the grounds of the difference in their ontological status. However, I would argue that Beloved is not unambiguously supernatural. There are enough clues in the novel for a "natural" reading and hence for a "legitimate" comparison between her and Denver. The ambiguity of Beloved's mode of existence, however, goes far beyond legitimating the comparison between Denver's success and Beloved's failure in crystallizing a self. This ambiguity is crucial both for the novel's problematization of the possibility of gaining access to reality and for its tentative retrieval of representation. Here again, as in the case of narrative levels, *Beloved* uses destabilizing modernist and postmodernist strategies to re-engage with reality.

Since 1990, when the first version of this chapter was written, numerous critics have explored Beloved's identity in ways that partly overlap with mine. I will therefore start by outlining the main directions of the later studies, subsequently sharpening my own emphases within this context. Many studies discuss the enigmatic title character as a double symbol, operating simultaneously on a personal (or psychological) and a collective level. On the personal level, Beloved is variously seen as a condensation of Sethe's daughter and her African mother (Horvitz 1989, 158); a projection of the needs and desires of the other characters (Wilt 1989, 161–62); the return of the repressed (Ferguson 1991, 113); "the incarnated memory of Sethe's guilt" (Rushdy 1992, 578); the pre-Oedipal child who desires a merger with her mother (Wyatt 1993, 480); and "all the babies in the womb" (Homans 1994, 10–11). On the collective level, most critics—with differences in nuance—interpret her as symbolic of "a whole lineage of people obliterated by slavery, beginning with the Africans who died on the Middle Passage" (Wyatt 1993, 474; see also Horvitz 1989, 157; Ferguson 1991, 115; Rushdy 1992, 571; Homans 1994, 10–11).

My own concern is much more elementary. I am puzzled by who Beloved is at the level of the events. An attempt to figure out the story seems to me logically and narratologically prior to symbolic interpretations, though it often invites these interpretations by the difficulties it presents. Is Beloved the flesh-and-blood reincarnation of Sethe's dead baby, the ghost returning as a person (a supernatural being), or a stranger who comes to 124 after horrendous tribulations, mistaking Sethe for her lost mother (a natural being)? Most critics explicitly or implicitly opt for one of the possibilities. Initially, reviewers conceived of Beloved as univocally supernatural (see Crouch 1987, Edwards 1987, Rumens 1987, and Thurman 1987). Many of the symbolic interpretations mentioned above take a similar view: Deborah Horvitz talks about "the powerful corporeal ghost" (1989, 157); Rebecca Ferguson, about "the supernatural at work in the 'world of common reality'" (1991, 113); and Ashraf Rushdy, about a "ghost" and a "reincarnation" (1992, 571). Elizabeth House flies in the face of this consensus by developing an equally univocal but opposed interpretation. She sees the novel as "a story of two probable instances of mistaken identity" (1990, 22). Beloved, according to her, is not a supernatural being but a young woman who herself suffered the horrors of slavery (ibid., 17) and who, haunted by the loss of her dead parents, comes to believe that Sethe is her mother. Analogously, Sethe's longing for her dead daughter makes her rather easily convinced that Beloved is the child she has lost (ibid., 22). The conflict between supernatural and natural interpretations seems to call for choice, but the novel renders choice impossible, offering supporting clues for both alternatives and maintaining an ambiguity that some critics recognize (e.g., Wilt 1990; FitzGerald 1993; Phelan 1993; Homans 1994) and which I would like to describe in detail now.

Many details dispersed throughout the novel support Beloved's identity as a supernatural, flesh-and-blood reincarnation of Sethe's dead baby. Most prominent perhaps is her name, which is not even a proper name. In the rebirth scene, it is Beloved who says her name, and Sethe's reaction is unnerving: "Sethe was deeply touched by her sweet name; the remembrance of glittering headstone made her feel especially kindly toward her" (53). This somewhat cryptic remark becomes clearer at other points in the novel where we learn that "Beloved" was the one word Sethe had engraved on the tombstone of her dead baby (5, 184), a word for which she had to pay by yielding her body to the engraver.[21] Another link between the returning Beloved and the dead baby is the "three vertical scratches on her forehead" (51), which Sethe later identifies as "my fingernail prints right there on your forehead for all the world to see. From when I held your head up, out in the

shed" (202–3). An even stronger connection is the scar on
Beloved's neck, identical to the cut caused by the handsaw in the
murder scene. The scar constitutes an indissoluble bond between
Sethe and Beloved, a bond Denver experiences as exclusion: "But
once Sethe had seen the scar, the tip of which Denver had been
looking at whenever Beloved undressed . . . once Sethe saw it, fin-
gered it and closed her eyes for a long time, the two of them cut
Denver out of the games" (239; see also 120, 176). Similarly bind-
ing are the earrings, about which Beloved inquires very soon after
her return: "Where your diamonds?" (58); and "Tell me your earrings" (63). "How did she know?" (ibid.) is both Sethe's and the
reader's question, for Beloved's insistent interest in the earrings
clearly suggests that she knew Sethe earlier. The earrings, we
learn—crystal, not diamonds—were given to Sethe by her Kentucky lady as a wedding present (58), and she kept them through
all her suffering. When she came to 124, Baby Suggs found them
(94), and "Sethe jingled the earrings for the pleasure of the crawling already? girl, who reached for them over and over again"
(ibid.). "Crawling already?" is an expression recurrently associated with the baby whom Sethe later murders, and Beloved's
questions about the earrings may therefore be interpreted as
memories of a far past to which she has now returned. She keeps
emphasizing that she has come back in order to see Sethe's face
(e.g., 75). (Incidentally, the earrings are no longer with Sethe, as
the jailer has taken them to prevent her from harming herself
[183].) The name, the scratches, the scar, and the earrings all lead
up to the final click of recognition, which comes when Sethe hears
Beloved softly humming a song Sethe herself had made up for her
children (176). Beloved's acquaintance with a song that "nobody
knows . . . but me and my children" (175) becomes for Sethe the
final confirmation of Beloved's identity as the dead baby come
back to life.

   That the dead baby who first returned as a ghost has now come
back in the flesh is unquestioningly accepted—though often re-

sented—by various characters in the novel, as is the supernatural character of her return. For example, Denver "was certain that Beloved was the white dress that had knelt with her mother in the keeping room, the true-to-life presence of the baby that had kept her company most of her life" (119); Paul D thinks, "But what if the girl was not a girl, but something in disguise?" (127); and Ella, who explicitly associates Beloved with the devil, "didn't mind a little communication between the two worlds [as in the case of ghosts] but this [a return in the flesh] was an invasion" (257).

The invasion, I am afraid, cannot be so unquestioningly accepted by the reader, not because of a modern skepticism about supernatural events but because of conflicting evidence within the novel. Contradictions focus on two details: the separation between Beloved and Sethe, and the presence (or absence) of an iron circle around Sethe's neck. Both in her monologue and elsewhere, Beloved remembers with acute pain how her mother jumped alone off a boat of dead and dying slaves on which they were crouching together: "they do not push her she goes in" (212; see also 75, 211–13). Sethe, on the other hand, has very different memories of the way she parted from her daughter (and sons) during the escape from Sweet Home: "When the signal for the train came, you all was the only ones ready. I couldn't find Halle or nobody . . . So I sent you all to the wagon with the woman who waited in the corn" (197–98; see also 9–10, 159, 191). And when Sethe reaches Baby Suggs and 124, her "crawling already? girl" is there, having been rescued as planned. The two versions of this crucial event also involve Sethe's earrings: According to Beloved, the earrings—the diamonds—were in the water Sethe jumped into (75, 211); according to Sethe—and it may be significant in this connection that she speaks of crystal rather than diamonds—they were with her until she reached 124.[22]

The second contradiction concerns the presence or absence of an iron circle around Sethe's neck.[23] Thus, Beloved: "The woman is there with the face I want the face that is mine . . . if I had the

teeth of the man who died on my face I would bite the circle
around her neck" (211). In retrospect, this can illuminate her
strange behavior and enigmatic explanation in the scene in the
Clearing where Denver accuses her of having tried to strangle
Sethe: "I kissed her neck. I didn't choke it. The circle of iron
choked it" (101). Confusingly, however, at no other point in the
novel is there any mention of an iron circle around Sethe's neck,
and it is hard to imagine that such a humiliating and painful experience would not have come up in Sethe's own memories.

These contradictions support a reading that may explain
Beloved's identity in a natural, rather than a supernatural, way. Is
it possible to imagine that Beloved is not Sethe's dead baby, not
Sethe's daughter at all, but the daughter of some other slave who
had an iron circle round her neck and who jumped off the slave
boat into the water, leaving her daughter behind, with an unquenchable yearning for her smile and her earrings? Is it then possible to imagine that the abandoned Beloved was taken over by
some white man for his own purposes, as Sethe believes (119),
and as Stamp Paid later suggests to Paul D: "Was a girl locked up
in the house with a whiteman over by Deer Creek. Found dead
last summer and the girl gone. Maybe that's her. Folks say he had
her in there since she was a pup" (235; see also 215, 241). Could it
be then that after the man's death Beloved ran away, and, remembering something her mother had whispered about a house (213),
she identifies it with 124, certain that she has come home to the
woman who had left her? If this is a possible story, how do we explain Sethe's, Denver's, and Beloved's conviction that the returning creature is Sethe's dead baby? It seems to me—and I am glad
to find a similar interpretation in House's essay—that the conviction can be explained by the overwhelming emotional hunger all
three share: Beloved's hunger for her mother, for love, for "the
join"; Sethe's hunger for her daughter, for expiation; Denver's
hunger for company, for love, for someone who will help her wait
for her daddy (208). This would be a non-supernatural version of

Beloved's story. And it is perhaps to leave room for such a reading that in the rebirth scene the extradiegetic narrator does not designate the returning creature as "Beloved," only as "the woman," thereby leaving her identity unverified.

Unlike House, I have no desire to suggest that the natural explanation is preferable to the supernatural one. On the contrary, I believe that the novel oscillates between these two alternatives in an insoluble ambiguity. In generic terms, and in Todorovian parlance, I am suggesting that the novel is neither Marvellous (as it would be in the supernatural reading) nor Strange (as it would be in the natural interpretation), but Fantastic (Todorov 1970).[24] In the language of James Phelan's rhetorical reader-response orientation, the phenomenon can be described as "the stubborn." As distinct from the difficult, which is "recalcitrance that yields to our explanatory efforts," the stubborn is "recalcitrance that will not yield" (1993, 714). _Beloved_ is, according to him, "a paradigm case of the stubborn" (ibid.). The distinction, as well as the characterization of Beloved as "stubborn," makes experiential sense, but (as Phelan knows) it is also open to criticism on account of its relativism: What is stubborn for one reader may be only difficult for another. A description of structures like ambiguity, paradox, and the Fantastic may be one way of grounding the stubborn in the text, although from Phelan's point of view, this may be too objective-sounding, too grounded in the text and not sufficiently attuned to the experience of reading. Whether we remain with "the stubborn" or prefer "ambiguity," Phelan is quite right that an encounter with the phenomenon shifts the interpretive task "from explicating it to explaining the purpose of its recalcitrance" (ibid., 715).

What, then, are the purposes of the ambiguity (or stubbornness) surrounding Beloved's mode of existence? One of Phelan's hypotheses is that the stubborn forces us to renounce a feeling of mastering the experience. "Us," in his essay, stands for "white male," and from this position he modestly says: "To presume mastery here would be to flaunt my hubris" (721). It seems to me that the impossibility of mastering such an emotionally wrenching experience is not confined to white male readers. For similar or different reasons, African American readers probably find Beloved just as stubborn as white readers do, and the horrors of slavery just as ungraspable or unmasterable.

This leads me to speculate that one purpose of the ambiguity of Beloved is to dramatize the difficulty of gaining access to and making accessible an unbearable reality. After listening to a presentation of an earlier version of this chapter at Princeton (in 1990), Morrison suggested that the Fantastic status of the title character may be a displacement of what seems to Morrison much more central and much more unbelievable (fantastic in a nontechnical sense), namely "the slavery stuff" (her own words).[25] Reformulated in my terms, the ambiguity can be said to enact both the representational impetus and the obstacles it encounters.

That the obstacle in this case is at least partly psychological is hinted at by the notion of displacement. Elaborating on this, I would claim that the oscillation between the sensation of unreality (Beloved is not a "real" person) and the insistence of the traumatic events in the present (she has, nevertheless, returned as a flesh-and-blood creature) is a performative representation of the response to trauma on the part of the characters, the overall narrator, the author, and the reader. From this perspective, the unbelievability can be seen as a manifestation of denial, a characteristic defense mechanism against trauma. The intrusion of the horror, its lifelike return, enacts the obsession that is the obverse of the self-defensive response. The possibility of representation is thus riddled with ambivalence.

A similar ambivalence emerges in relation to narration. Its strongest manifestation, perhaps, is the "contradiction" between the recurrent assertion in the novel's last chapter, "It was not a story to pass on" (274–75), and the fact that this is precisely the story the novel *has* passed on. Many critics have noticed not only the contradiction but also the ambiguity of the recurrent sentence. "Pass on" can mean both transmit and ignore (pass over). It combines acceptance and rejection, an injunction to remember and a recommendation to forget (see Henderson 1990, 83; Ferguson 1991, 123–24; Wyatt 1993, 484; Perez-Torres 1993, 691; Homans 1994, 11). Phelan suggests that the two meanings of "it was not a story to pass on" not only contrast with each other, but together they form a contrast between stories and reality. Thus, it was not a *story* to pass on, (my emphasis) "but it was something else, a *reality* to be confronted" (1993, 720; Phelan's emphasis). Like the implied opposition between story and reality, *Beloved*'s stubbornness is seen by Phelan as (among other things) a challenge on Morrison's part to treat the narrative as a species of history: "not a story to pass on, but a person whose multiplicity transcends any story that can be told about her. And here the importance of the fiction comes back: her story stands in for the millions and millions of other slaves, whose lives and deaths, though not passed on in story, are just as deep, just as emotionally wrenching, just as important—as hers" (ibid., 723). This reading illuminates a double ambiguity, that of the recurrent sentence and that of the title character, relating both to the larger historical dimension. At the same time, it creates a polarity between story and reality, opposites that, in my opinion, the novel renders equivalent and subjects to the same ambivalence. Like the extradiegetic narrator, the characters are conflicted about the possibility and desirability of narration. Paul D's locked tobacco tin, Denver's self-defensive deafness, and Sethe's and Baby Suggs's tacit verdict that the past is unspeakable are only a few examples of the incapacity to tell (and hear) that characterizes repression. Counterbalancing this, however, are the need and the desire to tell, often equating life and (life) story. Sethe muses: "Her story was bearable because it was his as well—to tell, to refine and tell again" (99), and Paul D finally returns to Sethe because "He wants to put his story next to hers" (273). The capacity to narrate against all odds is seen in this novel as a therapeutic—even if tentative—access to both self and reality.

No less important than the therapeutic need to narrate is the moral duty to tell, as the epigraph clearly implies:

> I will call them my people
> which were not my people;
> and her beloved,
> which was not beloved.
>   (Romans 9:25)[26]

Without diminishing the difficulties attending the enterprise, *Beloved* ultimately affirms narration as both a therapeutic necessity and a moral imperative, a way of constituting a self and protecting a cruel reality against a comfortable amnesia. The novel becomes a complex re-engagement with representation and subjectivity, a claiming of the unclaimed, which, according to Ricoeur, is the *raison d'être* of all storytelling: "We tell stories because in the last analysis human lives need to and merit being narrated. This remark takes on its full force when we refer to the necessity to save the history of the defeated and the lost. The whole history of suffering cries out for vengeance and calls for narrative" (1985, 62).

Conclusion

Through an analysis of five twentieth-century novels, I have suggested a new approach to representation and subjectivity and have outlined a map of changing attitudes toward these concepts in our time. The attempt to theorize *via* literature is, at least partly, a reaction against impositions of theoretical models on literary texts or reductions of literary texts to the status of examples. Such tendencies, which had their rationale (theory, it was believed, should be concerned with the general rather than the specific), were particularly pronounced in structuralist narratology (including my own past work) and have often led to an unfortunate severing of any living contact between poetics and literature. The proposed return to the texts is also motivated by a belief that literature is a mode of knowledge different from (but in no way inferior to) theory and philosophy. For this reason, a study of theoretical problems through an analysis of literary texts can yield insights impossible for a purely conceptual inquiry. Just as the approach treats philosophical problems from a defamiliarizing (hence refreshing) narratological angle, so does it open up narratology to questions generally considered outside its purview.

I wish to acknowledge openly, however, both the burden that this approach puts on the textual readings—the proof of that burden is in the reading—and the circularity involved in the procedure. While deriving my theoretical claims from the novels themselves, I have not come to the texts as a tabula rasa, and a reading of literature with certain conceptual concerns in mind necessarily implies some theoretical orientation. Theorizing through a limited number of novels also raises the question: Is the emergent theory valid only for these novels, or others similar to them, or is it more generally applicable? The question becomes doubly acute because the novels I discuss share a foregrounding of the problems with which my book is concerned and may therefore be said to be both too easily amenable to this kind of analysis and not typical enough of the novel genre. I counter this hypothetical objection by pointing out a potential virtue in what seems like a limitation. Rather than militating against their use for my purposes, the foregrounding of the conceptual problems by the texts I choose may bring what usually lies underneath to the surface. This argument could be taken a step further with the help of de Man's rebuttal of the category of "self-conscious literature" (on the grounds that all literature is). I believe, however, that there are degrees of self-consciousness and degrees of foregrounding, and that the approach I suggest may look more "spectacular" in relation to some texts than in relation to others. This brings me to the earlier question of applicability. To my mind, if the theory is valid, it is valid for all fictional narratives, though it may have different shapes, nuances, and degrees in different texts. While an empirical demonstration of such a claim is impracticable, given the infinite number of available narratives, future studies may usefully take up novels that do not foreground the issues, but also do not prevent them from emerging. A study focusing on the realist tradition of the nineteenth century may be of special interest in this context, both because this tradition tends to shun self-conscious display and because it often uses external (omniscient) narrators, who are less easily conceived of as subjects.

Because my theory emerges largely from within the novels, but can also reach beyond these five texts, a delicate balance is needed not only between textual and conceptual analysis, but also between theoretical and historical poetics. The desire to rehabilitate representation and rehumanize subjectivity has motivated my project as a whole. However, the diachronic study locates the novels at different points along the continuum: *Absalom, Absalom!* and *The Real Life of Sebastian Knight* are conflicted, in varying degrees, about both representation and subjectivity; *Thru* dismantles both; *Company* dismantles them but also tentatively regains them on a different level; and *Beloved* integrates the destabilization and yet glances beyond doubt to a new affirmation. The need to find the correct balance between my general argument and the location of each text on the historical map is a challenge I hope I have met.

I was attracted to twentieth-century novels both because the issues at stake have become particularly acute in our period (though they are by no means exclusive to it) and because of the analogy (as well as the mutual influence) between the transition punctuated by the novels and the conceptual trajectory of literary theory. I have attributed this homology to the cultural landscape of our period, but I am also aware of the shadow of circularity. Can the shift be located in the sequence of novels, or does it result from the changing theoretical orientations I bring to bear upon them? Unfortunately, the question seems to me unanswerable. Indeed, it is a variation on the age-old crux: Is x in the text, or in our reading of (or approach to) the text? That both questions cannot be answered definitively does not, however, render the asking futile. Among other things, it alerts us to the possibility that ours is a profession where one finds what one is looking for.

My book attempts to break away both from traditional views of representation and subjectivity and from their poststructuralist dismantling, whether in deconstruction or in Althusser- and Foucault-inspired theories of ideology. The project of rehabilitation is not meant as a regression to earlier positions but as a spiraling movement that integrates skepticism and yet glances beyond it. The glance beyond is effected by shifting the ground from reference and specularity to access achieved through narration. I play with various connotations of access so as to go through destabilization and entrapment within discursive constructs, but emphasize the final act of substitution as a reaching gesture that involves a convention-governed trust or faith.

The mobile stance informing my concept of an access-function is reinforced by the stress on narration, highlighting the act or process of production rather than the final product. This dynamic grasp of the issue has the advantage of going beyond most structuralist narratology. A question that immediately arises, however, is: Whose act of production? This book is concerned with narrators, though it does insert occasional references to authors when the texts foreground them. It seems to me, however, that a theory that attempts to go beyond a view of the narrator as a structural position to a consideration of his/her subjectivity should be able to open itself up to a similar treatment of authors. Whether approached as one of the voices in a Bakhtinian polyphony or as the agent whose act of production is responsible for the various fictional narrations, the reborn author will not be the same as the one whose death was so definitively announced. But it is clear to me that some rebirth is called for by a theory that spotlights narration. The distinction between the real and the implied author may be less radical than it seemed in the days of New Criticism and structuralism, since the real author is also in some sense implied. What we know about the author is drawn mainly from discourses by and about him or her (literary texts, letters, notes, memoirs by friends, etc.).[1] This is rather similar to the way the character-narrators in *Absalom, Absalom!* and *The Real Life of Sebastian Knight* try to interpret "reality" and the subjects inhabiting it: they read documents, listen to stories, infer, and create.

The narrators' transference-like repetition of the events they narrate confers further dynamism on the act of narration. The performative dimension that is explicitly dramatized in Quentin's and Shreve's reliving of Henry and Bon, as well as in V's transformation into Sebastian Knight (or vice versa), exists, I suggest, in every act of narration.

And in every act of reading. In *Absalom, Absalom!* the readers find themselves in a position analogous to Sutpen's victims', confronted with gaps, absences, and obscurities that impede the desire for intelligibility. Their attempts to figure out the story often involve imaginative invention, like the creation of a hypothetical scene between Quentin and Henry in which the principal secret is supposedly divulged. In *Beloved,* the readers' oscillation between a supernatural and a natural interpretation of the title character's identity is a performative repetition of the response to trauma by the characters and the overall narrator. What these texts dramatize explicitly may be implicitly true of narrators and readers in all texts: processing the text in the act of reading, the readers also "perform" it, experientially repeating the narrators' acts of production. My description of the access function of narration also applies to readers, as they gain access through a performative repetition of the processes of the text. They too operate a metaphoric credit card, with its institutionalized conventions and its trust-governed gesture of substitution.

"The reader is the writer and the writer the reader," says *Thru* (30) in an extreme formulation of what many theoreticians prefer to see as equivalence or complementarity. The centrality of listening or reading to the functioning of narration is obvious in the novels I discuss. The Quentin-Shreve collaboration in *Absalom, Absalom!* is a "happy marriage of speaking and hearing" (316) in which the narratee is just as active as the narrator. In *Beloved,* narration becomes most strongly creative, and most strongly a way of claiming ownership of the self, when it is shared with another (Denver with Beloved, Paul D with Sethe, on so on). And the lonely creature in *Company* devises a hearer to make both narration and company possible.

Equally kinetic are the transformations disrupting the stratification of narrative levels: subversion, interpenetration, reversibility, interchangeability, and mutual cancellations.[2] The same strategies, differently used, serve both the destabilization of representation and subjectivity and their rehabilitation. Thus, whereas the multiplication of narrative levels in *Absalom, Absalom!* and *The Real Life of Sebastian Knight* enacts a doubt about the possibility of reaching reality and constituting a self, in *Beloved* it operates as an access to both.

My analysis of representation and subjectivity through the concept of narration can be fruitfully linked to the current narrative turn in a variety of disciplines—historiography, psychoanalysis, sociology, communication studies, and jurisprudence. Although my book is concerned with fictional narration, it clearly stands to gain from the perceived continuity with extraliterary practices. I venture to say, however, that my perspective can also enrich these new orientations in at least two respects. The concept of narrative is often used in these disciplines to counter the notion of truth-claims or factuality. In *I, Pierre Rivière* (1978), Foucault tells the main event—the multiple murder—from various points of view and through various narrators, none of whom is more authoritative than the others. The result is, in many ways, similar to the novels I analyze here: a demystification of truth, a destabilization of reality, a questioning of event. Hayden White (1978) sees history as a species of narrative and classifies it under various tropes, using the concept of plot. Donald Spence (1982) speaks about "narrative truth" rather than "historical truth" in psychoanalysis. Difficulties with knowledge, reality, and the like have often led to an emphasis on the fictional status of (or fictional dimension in) historiography, psychoanalysis, and other disciplines.[3] Within these developments, narrative is also part of a reaction against theory, at least in its traditional acceptation as objective, verifiable, universal. Paradoxically, narrative theory is often used today in order to dislodge theory.

Obviously, I cannot do justice to these fascinating approaches here, nor can I broach a serious discussion of my agreements and disagreements with their assumptions and procedures. All I can do is suggest that the interface between them and the theory I have developed may give rise to a use of *narrative* (and even more, *narration*) that does not substitute for reality but offers a complex access to it. It may also help reestablish a contact between narrative and theory, where theory will be enriched by the specificity of narratives, while narratives will open up to a form of theorizing that grows out of them, integrates both destabilization and a dynamics of "visions and revisions," and yet gestures toward some kind of re-affirmation.

Appendix

The narratological terms used in this study are all borrowed from Gérard Genette's *Figures III,* and I will define them briefly for the sake of readers who may not be familiar with Genette's seminal book.[1] Narrative levels are a phenomenon of embedding, subordination, relations of containing/contained, or outside/inside, between the act of narration and the events narrated, as well as between various stories told in one text. The highest, or outermost, level is the one concerned with the narration of the events (or *diegesis*) and is therefore called *extradiegetic.* Immediately subordinate to the extradiegetic level is the *diegetic* level it narrates, that is, the events themselves. Events may include speech acts of narration, whether oral or written. Stories told by characters belonging to the diegetic level constitute a second-degree narrative, a *metadiegetic* level. Within this level additional stories may create a *meta-metadiegetic* level, and so on ad infinitum (at least in principle).

Sometimes the relations between narrative levels are those of analogy, that is, similarity and contrast. An analogy that verges on identity, making one level a kind of mirror or reduplication of another, is known by the term *mise en abyme.* The transition from one narrative level to another is in principle effected by the act of narration, which draws the reader's attention to the shift. Sometimes, however, the transition is not marked, and the discreteness of levels is transgressed. Characters from an inner story may, for example, address their narrator, or the "dear reader" may be asked to help a character accomplish a difficult task. The transgression of levels is known as *metalepsis.* In extreme cases it collapses completely the distinction between outside and inside, container and contained, narrating subject and narrated object, often resulting in a radical problematization of the border between reality and fiction.

Narration is by definition at a higher narrative level than the story it narrates. One classification of narrators therefore depends on the typology of narrative levels. The diegetic level is narrated by an extradiegetic narrator, the metadiegetic level by a diegetic (or intradiegetic) narrator, and the meta-metadiegetic level by a metadiegetic one.

Genette distinguishes between *narration* and *focalization* (formerly known as *point of view*). Succinctly put, his distinction is between speaking and seeing (where seeing is—at least in my interpretation—not restricted to the visual; cf. Rimmon-Kenan 1983, 71–85). A person, and by analogy, a narrative agent, is capable of both speaking and seeing, and even of doing both things at the same time—a state of affairs that facilitates the widespread confusion between the two activities. Moreover, it is almost impossible to speak without betraying some personal point of view, if only through the language used. But a person or a narrative agent is also capable of undertaking to tell what another person sees or has seen. Thus speaking and seeing, narration and focalization, may, but need not, be attributed to the same agent.

Notes

A Note on Terminology

1. See Cadava, Connor, and Nancy 1991 for the non-uniformity of various uses of *subject*. My account here and in the book itself may well be contested by other theoreticians.

Introduction

1. See "A Note on Terminology," above.

2. On the mutual generation of opposites in a different conceptual framework, see McCanles, 1975, 258.

3. Prendergast stresses both the connection between reference and a truth-claim and the problematic status of such a claim: "One can only refer to something that is held to exist in the world (or, in Frege's terms, something in the world about which statements possessing truth-value can be made)" (1986:62-3).

Chapter I

1. Ricoeur has argued that *mimesis* in Aristotle does not mean an imitation of reality but an imitation of plot, an "articulated signification of action" (1983, 88).

2. *Traditional* here refers to a humanistic cast of mind, not a historical period.

3. One should note that Smith rejects the two-level model of narrative *(fabula/sjužet)*, explicitly arguing against a chronological or logical priority of the events. But her "transactional" model implies a view that, in this respect, resembles the view she rejects.

4. For a similar description, see Bal 1984, 343–44.

5. Indeed, *Representations* is the name of a distinguished New Historicist periodical.

6. For a brief review of such tendencies, see Gagnier 1991. See also Derrida's present concern with agency, choice, and responsibility (1991).

7. As I have already suggested in the introduction, there are affinities between the question of representation in fiction and historiographical attempts to reconstruct a past—in spite of crucial distinctions between these discursive modes from other points of view (on some of the differences, see Cohn 1990, 775–804.)

8. De Lauretis makes a similar point about discourses on sexuality, emphasizing that the choice manifests an "investment," "something between an emotional commitment and a vested interest in the relative power (satisfaction, reward, payoff) which that position promises (but does not necessarily fulfill)" (1987, 6).

9. I transform what Bakhtin says in the negative about authoritative discourse into positive statements about its opposite, i.e. the internally persuasive discourse.

10. De Lauretis makes a similar claim for a view of the subject, which emerges from current debates within feminism (1987, 10).

11. Nor is Genette unaware of the possibility of problematization. His model describes various techniques that subvert neat categories.

Chapter 2

1. All references are to the Vintage edition of 1972.

2. I say "predominantly" because the narrator sometimes changes within a single chapter and is sometimes unclear or ambiguous. I take up some problematic examples below.

3. On narrative perspective or point of view in *Absalom, Absalom!* see Waggoner 1966, 175–85; Levins 1970, 35–47; Lind 1973, 272–97; Brooks 1984, 286–312; Kauffman 1986, 241–77; Toker 1993, 152–84.

4. See also pages 178, 181, 311, 326, 327.

5. See also pages 27–28, 147.

6. See also pages 27, 140, 145.

7. See also pages 296–99, 300, 310–11, 314–15, 316–18, 319–20, 337–38, and 342–45 for scenes Shreve has probably not heard from Quentin.

8. Note that the few occasions on which Shreve does agree with Mr. Compson only emphasize the overall disagreement. For example, "And maybe this was one place where your old man was right" (342; see also 343, 374).

9. For a more detailed analysis of conflicting views of the possible motives for the murder see Rimmon-Kenan 1978, f10–f12.

10. Felman's by now classical analysis of James's *The Turn of the Screw* (1977, 94–207) dwells on the reader's repetition of the mistakes of the characters.

11. For an emphasis on a literal reading of this statement as a hint that Bon is indeed Sutpen's son, see Toker 1993, 159–60.

12. For an interesting interpretation of Rosa as *the* lover in *Absalom, Absalom!* see Kauffman 1986, 241–77.

13. See Irwin 1975, 113–20, and McPherson 1987, 432–33, 438, for a view of narration as a power struggle.

14. Rosa is an exception, but she is more peripheral to the events than Sutpen, Henry, Bon, and Judith. Kauffman's emphasis on Rosa's values as those affirmed by the novel may partly explain why she *is* made a narrator.

15. See 353 of the novel for a similar statement about the mysterious workings of the "rapport of blood" between Sutpen, Henry, and Bon. Kauffman 1986 and McPherson 1987 offer detailed analyses of the "touch of flesh with flesh."

16. Note that this is a different way of looking at the issue of nonverbal communication discussed earlier.

17. See Irwin 1975, 28, 78, and elsewhere for an explanation of the Henry and Bon that Quentin creates. Irwin relies for his explanation on *The Sound and the Fury*. Not all critics would agree with such a conflation of two novels.

18. For analysis of additional examples, see Brodsky 1978.

19. For additional comments on this italicized segment see Brodsky 1978, 252 and Toker 1993, 153–54.

20. Barthes (1970) sees this as part of the bourgeois emphasis on private property.

21. To support her hypothesis, Toker also adduces the occurrence of paralepses (the imparting of information that the character-narrator could not have) and of insights that are improbable from the point of view of the character concerned. I find Toker's view difficult to accept, since Rosa, Mr. Compson, Quentin, and Shreve *do* tell their versions of the story, often in the first person, and always to a narratee. By definition, the one who tells is a narrator, whereas the focalizer is the one who perceives the events or through whose eyes we perceive them (cf. Genette 1972, 203). The combination of an extradiegetic narrator with a character-focalizer would take the form of third-person narration through the prism (but not the voice) of a character, as, for example, in James's *The Ambassadors*. This is clearly not the case in *Absalom, Absalom!*

22. While Waggoner's view can be supported by the initial image of the two Quentins (9), as well as by the snow on Shreve's overcoat sleeve (173), it remains inconclusive, somewhat undermined by various shifters indicating the here and now of the first five chapters (e.g., 14).

23. See also page 367.

24. See also pages 335, 345, 346, 351.

25. This is said about Rosa, but it can, I think, also apply to the narrative efforts of the other characters. Kauffman takes the position that Rosa's female discourse succeeds where the male discourses fail.

26. Other analogies, e.g., the parallelism between Bon's status as a phantom in the lives of the various characters and the shadow realities created by narration were discussed above in a different context.

27. My emphasis on the success of the Quentin-Shreve creation requires some reservation, since at the end of the novel Quentin is close to a nervous breakdown.

Chapter 3

1. All references are to the Penguin edition of 1971.

2. See Rimmon-Kenan, 1976, 506–11 for an attempt to show how the novel blocks the possibility of choosing between the hypotheses.

3. This is the beginning from the point of view of the chronology of the story, not from that of the disposition of events in the text.

4. Note the difference between a literal identification (Abeson and Nosebag) and a figurative one (V and Sebastian).

5. The expression "false scent" is used in connection both with *Success* (80) and with V's meeting with Goodman (50).

6. Uncle Black, named after the black chess figure, could write his name upside down, and the expression "upside down" recurs, albeit in a completely different context, in *The Doubtful Asphodel:* "physical growth considered upside down" (148).

7. Note the phonetic similarity of "Nussbaum" and "Nosebag."

8. For more analogies see Fromberg 1967, 434–36; Nicol 1967, 87–93; Bader 1972, 17–24; Rimmon-Kenan 1976, 497–501.

9. Cf. Stuart 1968, 325.

10. Note the repetition of *v* in "velvet."

11. Note how the use of aural or visual alliteration, e.g., "sibilant slope" and "winding"—"writing," enacts what it talks about.

12. In some sense it really does, since it is the author who decides to "kill" the character, but this causal relationship is denied in the quoted passage by the impression of unwittingness: the pause was fatal; it accidentally caused the man's death.

Chapter 4

1. All references are to the Hamish Hamilton edition of 1975.

2. Larissa is listed in the schedule as teaching "The Novel as Intentional Object" (21), and her views are stated in the minutes of the staff meeting (96). Armel writes a letter to Larissa during another staff meeting (26); his comments appear on students' compositions (48, 73, 74); and one of his courses, "The Beginnings of Narrative," is listed in the file of a student named Saroja (34).

3. Note the ambiguity here: (a) she was producing Armel; (b) Armel was producing the text.

4. "Textasy" is the title of the first article published on *Thru* (Kafalenos 1980, 43–46).

5. Note also the repetition of the title word, though spelled conventionally, in this sentence.

6. Birch (1994) gives an excellent analysis of the intertextual play with Greimas and Lacan.

7. In an interview, Brooke-Rose said that, for her, the real theme of *Thru* is castration (1976, 11), but she went on immediately to refer to the "découpage of reality" by "the very act of using language" (11–12), i.e., castration in a figurative, metalinguistic sense.

8. For a Lacanian interpretation of the shattering of the narrative voice into a multitude of surrogate "bearers of the tale," see Birch (1994).

Chapter 5

1. All references are to the Grove Press edition of 1980.

2. Here and elsewhere, Booth also wonders about the identity of the various addressers and addressees, but he does not analyse it in terms of narrative levels (1983, 445, 447).

3. I borrow this felicitous expression from the title of a 1994 book by Schwab.

4. Quotations from this text here and elsewhere in the chapter are from Beckett's *Molloy, Malone Dies, The Unnamable* (New York: Grove Weidenfeld, 1965). The French original was published in 1952.

5. A similar fusion of two characters (if they are two) is dramatized in Nabokov's *The Real Life of Sebastian Knight*. There too the merging is reinforced by a game of letters. This happens, we remember, when V, the narrator's initial, is inserted into Sebastian's name in Dr. Starov's telegram.

6. See also Locatelli's analysis, 1990:182 and elsewhere.

Chapter 6

1. See, for example, the near oxymoron in "the two did the best they could to *create* what *really happened*" (78). All references are to the Signet New American Library edition of 1987.

2. For this reason I use "self" (rather than "subject") in my analysis of *Beloved*.

3. For a different discussion of the place of *Beloved* in postmodernism see Perez-Torres 1993, 659–707.

4. By near levels I mean phenomena that do not constitute narrative levels in the strict sense (i.e., when an object of narration becomes the narrating subject of a second-degree narrative) but are close to it in effect. An example is the embedding of second-degree focalization in a narrative whose narrator does not change.

5. On the difference between quoted and autonomous interior monologues see Cohn 1978, 14–15.

6. For a definition of *scene* both as detailed narration and as dialogue, see Rimmon-Kenan 1983, 54–55.

7. "First narrative" is Genette's term for the level narrated by the extradiegetic narrator (1972, 239). Most readers, of course, do not formulate their experience in these narratological terms.

8. The passage that follows this sentence is indeterminate as to voice and perspective. Is it told and focalized by the narrator, by Denver, by Sethe? Even tags like "said Sethe," while making it seem like her narration, can be construed as Denver's memories of her words or as the extradiegetic narrator's quotation of what Sethe said.

9. The near-identity between Sethe's age when giving birth to Denver and Denver's age when narrating her birth also diminishes the sense of distance.

10. Much later, after discovering Beloved's identity, Sethe associates the drinking of water with Beloved's behavior as a baby: "I would have known who you were right away because the cup after cup of water you drank proved and connected to the fact that you dribbled clear spit on my face the day I got to 124" (200).

In addition to the parallels, there is also a local contrast in the resurrection scene between Sethe's voiding and Beloved's drinking of water.

11. Beloved's return is not the only example in the novel of dead things coming back to life. Sethe returns to (sexual) life thanks to Paul D, while Paul D himself is reawakened by Beloved ("She moved him"). In both cases the return hurts.

12. Although this is narrated before the traumatic question, it follows it in the chronology of the story.

13. Even Sethe is said to have shaped the story, so there is creation in

every re-creation. There is a similarity between this view of narration as creation and, more important, creation by two, and the Quentin-Shreve narration in *Absalom, Absalom!*

14. The nonexistence of time for Beloved can also explain the difficulty of locating her two monologues in the temporal scheme of the novel: Do they occur in the narrative present? At the time of the separation from Sethe? Or at the time of their re-union? There are clues to support each possibility, and no decisive way of choosing among them.

15. Cf. "I am going to be in pieces" (212) and "after the bottoms of my feet swim away from me" (213). For a discussion of fragmentation see Ferguson 1991, 115.

16. "The body in pieces" *(le corps morcelé)* is a Lacanian expression (1966, 94) that I borrow without dwelling on all its implications for *Beloved*. The implications are highly interesting, but they lead in a direction that would blur the focus of this discussion.

17. Without love, there is a threat of disintegration. Therefore, when Paul D returns to Sethe after having left her, and wants to rub her feet, she thinks about the possibility of his washing her: "Will he do it in sections? . . . And if he bathes her in sections, will the parts hold?" (272).

18. Henderson uses the same pun in a slightly different context (1990, 71, 72).

19. For analyses of this lack of dissociation in terms of object-relations psychoanalysis, see Schapiro 1991 and FitzGerald 1993. See also Wyatt 1993 for a Kristevan analysis of this phenomenon and a coining of the notion of a maternal symbolic.

20. Her need to have someone who would want her and would say her name is dramatized in the love scene with Paul D, where she asks him to touch her "on the inside part" and call her name (116). Note also that Beloved's making love to her mother's lover and later becoming pregnant (presumably) by him is one more manifestation of Sethe and Beloved as, in some sense, doubles. Interestingly, in order to break the spell Beloved has on him, Paul D says to Sethe that he would like to have a baby with *her*.

21. The word *Beloved* is half of the preacher's speech in the funeral ("Dearly Beloved"), and Beloved's name thus comes from the discourse

of the other. Names in this novel are an interesting subject in their own right, deserving a separate analysis.

22. House interprets the diamonds in the water as reflections of the sun (1990, 21).

23. Rather than conflicting evidence, House sees the differences concerning the iron collar as changes in Beloved's perception of her mother during the sea voyage (1990, 19).

24. See McHale 1987, 74–76, for a distinction between the epistemological fantastic that characterizes modernism and the ontological fantastic operative in postmodernism.

25. In earlier interviews Morrison had said that she meant Beloved to be credible as a flesh-and-blood reincarnation of the dead baby. I am flattered that she agreed in retrospect that both readings are possible.

26. According to House, the epigraph is a hint that the returning young woman is not the baby called Beloved (1990, 22).

Conclusion

1. I am grateful to Moshe Ron for many discussions of this subject.

2. Such dynamic transformations are already implicit in Genette 1972.

3. For a vehement resistance to such stretching of boundaries, see Cohn 1990, 775–804.

Appendix

1. For convenience, I rely on my own explanations of Genette's terms in Rimmon-Kenan 1983.

Bibliography

Alter, Robert. 1984. *Motives for Fiction*. Cambridge, Mass.: Harvard University Press.

Althusser, Louis. 1969. *For Marx*. Harmondsworth: Penguin Books.

———. 1971. *Lenin and Philosophy and Other Essays*. London: New Left Books.

Arthur, Kateryna. 1987. "Texts for Company." In *Beckett's Later Fiction and Drama: Texts for Company*, ed. James Acheson and Kateryna Arthur, 136–44. London: Macmillan.

Auerbach, Erich. 1953. *Mimesis: Representation of Reality in Western Literature*. Princeton: Princeton University Press.

Bader, Julia. 1972. *Crystal Land: Artifice in Nabokov's English Novels*. Berkeley: University of California Press.

Bakhtın, M. M. 1981. *The Dialogic Imagination*. Austin: University of Texas Press.

Bal, Mieke. 1984. "The Rhetoric of Subjectivity." *Poetics Today* 5:337–76.

———. 1990. "The Point of Narratology." *Poetics Today* 11:727–53.

Barthes, Roland. 1970. *S/Z*. Paris: Seuil.

———. 1972. "To Write: An Intransitive Verb." In *The Structuralists: From Marx to Lévi-Strauss,* ed. Richard T. De George and M. Fernande. New York: Doubleday, Anchor Books.

———. 1974. *S/Z*. New York: Hill and Wang.

Beckett, Samuel. 1980. *Company*. New York: Grove Press.

Belsey, Catherine. 1980. *Critical Practice*. London: Methuen.

Bender, John. 1987. *Imagining the Penitentiary: Fiction and the Architecture of the Mind in Eighteenth-Century England.* Chicago: University of Chicago Press.

Birch, Sarah. 1994. *Christine Brooke-Rose and Contemporary Fiction.* Oxford: Oxford University Press.

Booth, Wayne. 1961. *The Rhetoric of Fiction.* 2d ed., 1983. Chicago: University of Chicago Press.

Brater, Enoch. 1983. "The *Company* Beckett Keeps: The Shape of Memory and One Fablist's Decay of Lying." In *Samuel Beckett: Humanistic Perspectives,* ed. Morris Beja, S. E. Gontarski, and Pierre Astier, 157–71. Columbus: Ohio State University Press.

Brodsky, Claudia. 1978. "The Working of Narrative in *Absalom, Absalom!*" *Amerikastudien/American Studies* 23:240–59.

Brooke-Rose, Christine. 1975. *Thru.* London: Hamish Hamilton.

————. 1976. Interview conducted by David Hayman and Keith Cohen. *Review of Contemporary Literature* 17:1–23.

Brooks, Cleanth. 1963. *William Faulkner: Yoknopatawpha County.* New Haven: Yale University Press.

Brooks, Peter. 1984. *Reading for the Plot.* New York: Knopf.

Bruffee, K. A. 1973. "Form and Meaning in Nabokov's *The Real Life of Sebastian Knight:* An Example of Elegaic Romance." *Modern Language Quarterly* 34:180–90.

Cadava, Eduardo, Peter Connor, and Jean-Luc Nancy. 1991. *Who Comes after the Subject?* New York: Routledge.

Cixous, Hélène. 1974. "The Character of 'Character.'" *New Literary History* 5:383–402.

Cohn, Dorrit. 1978. *Transparent Minds: Narrative Modes for Presenting Consciousness in Fiction.* Princeton: Princeton University Press.

————. 1990. "Signposts of Fictionality: A Narratological Perspective." *Poetics Today* 11:775–804.

Crouch, Stanley. 1987. "Aunt Medea." *New Republic,* 19 October, 42.

Culler, Jonathan. 1981. *The Pursuit of Signs: Semiotics, Literature, Deconstruction.* London: Routledge and Kegan Paul.

————. 1982. *On Deconstruction.* Ithaca: Cornell University Press.

de Lauretis, Teresa. 1987. *Technologies of Gender: Essays on Theory, Film, and Fiction.* Bloomington: Indiana University Press.

de Man, Paul. 1979. *Allegories of Reading: Figural Language in*

Rousseau, Nietzsche, Rilke, and Proust. New Haven: Yale University Press.

Derrida, Jacques. 1972. *La Dissemination.* Paris: Seuil.

———. 1976. *Of Grammatology.* Baltimore: Johns Hopkins University Press.

———. "Eating Well: An Interview with Jacques Derrida." In *Who Comes after the Subject?,* ed. Eduardo Cadava, Peter Connor, and Jean-Luc Nancy. New York: Routledge.

Edwards, Thomas R. 1987. "Ghost Story." *New York Review of Books,* 5 November, 18.

Escher, M. C. 1972. *The Graphic Work of M. C. Escher.* Trans. John E. Brigham. London: Pan/Ballantine.

Ewen, Joseph. 1974. "Writer, Narrator, and Implied Author" (in Hebrew; English abstract pp. vii–ix). *Ha-sifrut* 18–19:137–63.

Faulkner, William. 1972. *Absalom! Absalom!* New York: Vintage Books.

Felman, Shoshana. 1978. "Turning the Screw of Interpretation." *Yale French Studies* 55/56:94–207.

Ferguson, Rebecca. 1991. "History, Memory and Language in Toni Morrison's *Beloved.*" In *Feminist Criticism: Theory and Practice,* ed. Susan Sellers. New York: Harvester Wheatsheaf.

FitzGerald, Jennifer. 1993. "Selfhood and Community: Psychoanalysis and Discourse in *Beloved.*" *Modern Fiction Studies* 39:669–87.

Foucault, Michel. 1969. *L'Archéologie du savoir.* Paris: Gallimard.

———. 1970. *The Order of Things.* London: Tavistock.

———. 1972. *The Archeology of Knowledge.* London: Tavistock.

———. 1978a. *I, Pierre Rivière, Having Slaughtered My Mother, My Sister, and My Brother.* Harmondsworth: Peregrine.

———. 1978b. "Politics and the Study of Discourse." *Ideology and Consciousness* 3:7-26.

———. 1979a. *Discipline and Punish: The Birth of the Prison.* New York: Pantheon Books.

———. 1979b. "What Is an Author?" *Screen* 20:13–33.

Freud, Sigmund. 1958. "Remembering, Repeating, and Working Through." In *The Standard Edition of the Complete Psychological Works of Sigmund Freud,* ed. James Strachey. London: Hogarth Press and the Institute of Psychoanalysis.

Fromberg, Susan. 1967. "The Unwritten Chapters in *The Real Life of Sebastian Knight.*" *Modern Fiction Studies* 13:427–42.

Fultz, Lucie. 1991. "Narrating Motherhood in Bondage: Toni Morrison's *Beloved.*" Paper presented at the Conference of the Society for the Study of Narrative Literature, June, Nice.

Gagnier, Regina. 1991. *Subjectivities: A History of Self-Representation in Britain, 1832–1920.* New York: Oxford University Press.

Genette, Gérard. 1972. *Figures III.* Paris: Seuil.

Goldman, Anne E. 1990. "'I Made the Ink': (Literary) Production and Reproduction in *Dessa Rosa* and *Beloved.*" *Feminist Studies* 16:313–30.

Harrison, Bernard. 1991. *Inconvenient Fictions: Literature and the Limits of Theory.* New Haven: Yale University Press.

Henderson, Mae G. 1990. "Toni Morrison's *Beloved:* Re-Membering the Body as Historical Text." In *Comparative American Identities: Race, Sex and Nationality in the Modern Text,* ed. Hortense J. Spillers, 62–86. New York: Routledge.

Homans, Margaret. 1994. "Feminist Fictions and Feminist Theories of Narrative." *Narrative* 2:3–16.

Horvitz, Deborah. 1989. "Narrative Ghosts: Possession and Depossession in *Beloved.*" *Studies in American Fiction* 17:157–67.

House, Elizabeth. 1990. "Toni Morrison's Ghost: The Beloved Who Is Not Beloved." *Studies in American Fiction* 18:17–26.

Irwin, John T. 1975. *Doubling and Incest/Repetition and Revenge.* Baltimore: Johns Hopkins University Press.

Iser, Wolfgang. 1989. "The Play of the Text." In his *Prospecting: From Reader Response to Literary Anthropology.* Baltimore: Johns Hopkins University Press.

———. 1993. *The Fictive and the Imaginary: Charting Literary Anthropology.* Baltimore: Johns Hopkins University Press.

Jameson, Frederic. 1980. *The Political Unconscious: Narrative as a Socially Symbolic Act.* Ithaca: Cornell University Press.

Jewinski, Ed. 1990. "Beckett's *Company,* Post-Structuralism, and Mimatologique." In *Rethinking Beckett: A Collection of Critical Essays,* ed. Lance St. John Butler and Robin J. Davis, 141–59. London: Macmillan.

Johnson, Barbara. 1978. "The Frame of Reference: Poe, Lacan, Derrida." *Yale French Studies* 55/56:457–505.

Kafalenos, Emma. 1980. "Textasy: Christine Brook-Rose's *Thru*." *International Fiction Review* 7:43–46.

Kauffman, Linda S. 1986. *Discourses of Desire, Gender, Genre, and Epistolary Fictions*. Ithaca: Cornell University Press.

Krause, David. 1984. "Reading Bon's Letter and Faulkner's *Absalom, Absalom!*" *PMLA* 99:225–41.

Lacan, Jacques. 1966. *Ecrits I*. Paris: Points.

Laing, R. D. 1960. *The Divided Self*. London: Tavistock.

Lawrence, D. H. 1914. Letter to Edward Garnett. In *The Letters of D. H. Lawrence,* ed. Aldous Huxley (1932). London: Heinemann.

Levins, Lynn Gartell. 1970. "The Four Narrative Perspectives in *Absalom, Absalom!*" *PMLA* 85:35–47.

Lind, Ilse Dusoir. 1973. "The Design and Meaning of *Absalom, Absalom!*" In *William Faulkner: Four Decades of Criticism,* ed. Linda Welshimer Wagner, 272–97. East Lansing: Michigan State University Press.

Locatelli, Carla. 1990. *Unwording the World: Samuel Beckett's Prose Works after the Nobel Prize*. Philadelphia: University of Pennsylvania Press.

MacIntyre, Alasdair. 1984. *After Virtue*. Notre Dame: University of Notre Dame Press.

McCanles, Michael F. 1975. *Dialectical Criticism and Renaissance Literature*. Berkeley and Los Angeles: University of California Press.

McHale, Brian. 1987. *Postmodernist Fiction*. London: Routledge.

McPherson, Karen. 1987. "*Absalom, Absalom!*: Telling Scratches." *Modern Fiction Studies* 33:431–50.

Mead, George Herbert. 1934. *Mind, Self, and Society*. Chicago: University of Chicago Press.

Miller, D. A. 1988. *The Novel and the Police*. Berkeley: University of California Press.

Morrison, Toni. 1987. *Beloved*. New York: Signet.

Nabokov, Vladimir. 1967. *The Eye*. New York: Pocket Books.

———. 1971. *The Real Life of Sebastian Knight*. Harmondsworth: Penguin.

Nicol, Charles. 1967. "The Mirrors of Sebastian Knight." In *Nabokov: The Man and His Work,* ed. L. S. Dembo, 85–94. Madison: University of Wisconsin Press.

Perez-Torres, Rafael. 1993. "Knitting and Knotting the Narrative Thread—*Beloved* as Post-Modern Novel." *Modern Fiction Studies* 39:659–707.

Phelan, James. 1993. "Toward a Rhetorical Reader-Response Criticism: The Difficult, the Stubborn, and the Ending of *Beloved.*" *Modern Fiction Studies* 39:709–28.

Pilling, John. 1982. "Review Article: 'Company' by Samuel Beckett." *Journal of Beckett Studies* 7:127–31.

Prendergast, Christopher. 1986. *The Order of Mimesis.* Cambridge: Cambridge University Press.

Ricoeur, Paul. 1983. *Temps et récit.* Paris: Seuil.

———. 1985. *Time and Narrative.* Chicago: University of Chicago Press.

———. 1991a. "Life in Quest of Narrative." In *On Paul Ricoeur: Narrative and Interpretation,* ed. David Wood. New York: Routledge.

———. 1991b. "Narrative Identity." In *On Paul Ricoeur: Narrative and Interpretation,* ed. David Wood. New York: Routledge.

———. 1992. *Oneself as Another.* Chicago: University of Chicago Press.

Riffaterre, Michael. 1984. "Intertextual Representation: On Mimesis as Interpretive Discourse." *Critical Inquiry* 11:141–62.

Rimmon-Kenan, Shlomith. 1976. "Problems of Voice in Vladimir Nabokov's *The Real Life of Sebastian Knight.*" *Poetics and Theory of Literature (PTL)* 1:489–512.

———. 1978. "From Reproduction to Production: The Status of Narration in Faulkner's *Absalom, Absalom!*" *Degrés* 16:f–f16.

———. 1982. "Ambiguity and Narrative Levels: Christine Brooke-Rose's *Thru.*" *Poetics Today* 3:21–32.

———. 1983. *Narrative Fiction: Contemporary Poetics.* London: Methuen.

Ron, Moshe. 1981. "Free Indirect Discourse, Mimetic Language Games and the Subject of Fiction." *Poetics Today* 2:17–39.

Ross, Stephen M. 1979. "'Voice' in Narrative Texts: The Example of *As I Lay Dying.*" *PMLA* 94:300–310.

Rumens, Carol. 1987. "Shades of the Prison House." *Times Literary Supplement,* 16–22 October, 1135.

Rushdy, Ashraf H. A. 1992. "Daughters Signifyin(g) History: The Example of Toni Morrison's *Beloved." American Literature* 64:567–97.

Russell, Bertrand, and Alfred North Whitehead. 1964. *The Principles of Mathematics.* Cambridge: Cambridge University Press.

Sarraute, Nathalie. 1956. *L'Ere du soupçon.* Paris: Gallimard.

Schapiro, Barbara. 1991. "The Bends of Love and the Boundaries of Self in Toni Morrison's *Beloved." Contemporary Literature* 32:194–210.

Scholes, Robert. 1980. "Language, Narrative, and Anti-Narrative." *Critical Inquiry* 7:204–12.

Schwab, Gabrielle. 1994. *Subjects without Selves: Transitional Texts in Modern Fiction.* Cambridge, Mass.: Harvard University Press.

Segal, Ora. "Beckett's *Company:* A Fictionalizing Process." Manuscript.

Seltzer, Mark. 1984. *Henry James and the Art of the Novel.* Ithaca: Cornell University Press.

Smith, Barbara Herrnstein. 1980. "Narrative Versions, Narrative Theories." *Critical Inquiry* 7:213–36.

Smith, Peter Duval, and Vladimir Nabokov. 1962. "Vladimir Nabokov on His Life and Work." *The Listener* 68:856.

Spariosu, Mihai. 1982. *Literature, Mimesis, and Play: Essays in Literary Theory.* Tübingen: Günter Narr Verlag.

Spence, Donald. 1982. *Narrative Truth and Historical Truth.* New York: Norton.

Spillers, Hortense J. 1991. "The Politics of Narrative: Passing It On." Paper presented at the Conference of the Society for the Study of Narrative Literature, June, Nice.

Stuart, Dabney. 1968. "*The Real Life of Sebastian Knight:* Angles of Perception." *Modern Language Quarterly* 29:312–28.

Taylor, Charles. 1989. *Sources of the Self.* Cambridge, Mass.: Harvard University Press.

Thiher, Allen. 1984. *Words in Reflection: Modern Language Theory and Postmodern Fiction.* Chicago: University of Chicago Press.

Thurman, Judith. 1987. "A House Divided." *New Yorker,* 2 November, 178.

Todorov, Tzvetan. 1970. *Introduction à la littèrature fantastique.* Paris: Seuil.

Toker, Leona. 1993. *Eloquent Reticence: Withholding Information in Fictional Narrative.* Lexington: University Press of Kentucky.

Veeser, Aram H., ed. 1989. *The New Historicism.* New York: Routledge.

Waggoner, Hyatt. 1966. "Past as Present: *Absalom, Absalom!*" In *Faulkner: A Collection of Critical Essays,* ed. Robert Penn Warren. Englewood Cliffs, N.J.: Prentice Hall.

White, Hayden. 1978. *Tropics of Discourse.* Baltimore: Johns Hopkins University Press.

Wilt, Judith. 1990. *Abortion, Choice, and Contemporary Fiction.* Chicago: University of Chicago Press.

Woolf, Virginia. 1925. "Modern Fiction." In *The Common Reader.* London: Hogarth Press.

Wyatt, Jean. 1993. "Giving Body to the Word: The Maternal Symbolic in Toni Morrison's *Beloved.*" *PMLA* 108:474–88.

Index

The Theory and Interpretation of Narrative Series

James Phelan and Peter J. Rabinowitz, Editors

Because the series editors believe that the most significant work in narrative studies today contributes both to our knowledge of specific narratives and to our understanding of narrative in general, studies in the series typically offer interpretations of individual narratives and address significant theoretical issues underlying those interpretations. The series does not privilege any one critical perspective but is open to work from any strong theoretical position.